DRIVING TEST

PRACTICAL AND THE HIGHWAY CODE

QUESTIONS
AND ANSWERS

by
Linda Hatswell B Ed (Hons)
AA driving school

Revised by
Sue Hubbard

Business Development Manager
AA driving school

Published by AA Publishing
(a trading name of Automobile Association Developments Limited,
whose registered office is Fanum House, Basing View, Basingstoke, Hampshire RG21 4EA
Registered number 1878835).
© Automobile Association Developments Limited 2003
Reprinted September 2003
Reprinted 2004 (twice)
Reprinted 2005 (twice)

A catalogue record for this book is available from the British Library.

ISBN - 10: 0 - 7495 - 3994 -1

ISBN - 13: 978 - 0 - 7495 - 3994 - 8

A02883

Originally published as the Driving Test Practical. First edition edited by Susan Gordon
Revised edition edited by Jane Gregory

Printed in China

www.theAA.com/bookshop

Visit **www.highwaycode.gov.uk** for all the latest
information on The Highway Code.

Foreword

You want to pass the driving test and take advantage of the freedom and mobility that driving a car can give you. Do the following three things and you will achieve your objective – passing the test.

1. Learn and understand the **skills** of driving by taking lessons from a trained and fully qualified driving instructor.

2. Acquire the **knowledge** of the rules through your instructor and by studying *The Highway Code*. A key element of learning is to test and reinforce your knowledge. This book is specially designed for this purpose.

3. Take the right **attitude.** No one is a 'natural' or a 'perfect' driver. All drivers make mistakes. Be careful, courteous and considerate to all other road users.

The fact that you are using this book shows that you have the right attitude to learning to drive. So, remember, acquire the **skills,** the **knowledge** and the right **attitude** and you will pass the test!

CONTENTS

CONTENTS

INTRODUCTION

by Sue Hubbard

Business Development Manager, AA The Driving School

GETTING A PROVISIONAL LICENCE

The driving licence is issued as a two-part document: a photo card and paper counterpart. So that you can legally begin learning to drive, at the appropriate date, you must have the correct licence documents.

Take time to read the instructions provided and take special care when completing all the necessary forms. Many licences cannot be issued for the required date because of errors or omissions on the application forms. You will have to provide a proof of identity such as a passport; make sure you have all the documents needed.

Make your application in good time; this can be as much as two months before it is required – for example, for a 17th birthday.

CHOOSING AN INSTRUCTOR

It is recommended that you learn with an Approved Driving Instructor (ADI). Only an ADI may legally charge for providing tuition.

Choose an instructor or driving school by asking friends or relatives whom they recommend. Price is important, so find out whether there are any discounts for blocks or courses of lessons paid in advance; if you decide to pay in

advance, make sure the driving school is reputable. If lesson prices are very low, ask yourself 'why?' Check how long the lesson will last. And don't forget to ask about the car you'll be learning to drive in. Is it modern and reliable? Is it insured? Has it dual controls?

The AA has a driving school that only uses fully qualified driving instructors, who are all familiar with the Practical and Theory Test. You can ring for details on 0800 60 70 80 or visit the website at www.theAA.com.

THE HIGHWAY CODE

The Highway Code is essential reading for all drivers not just those learning to drive. It sets out all the rules for good driving, as well as the rules for other road users, such as pedestrians and motorcycle riders. When you have learnt the rules you will be will be able to answer most of the questions in the Theory Test and be ready to start learning the driving skills you will need to pass your Practical Test. You will find the complete Highway Code at the back of this book for your reference.

TOWARDS THE DRIVING TEST

The driving test is in two parts, the Theory Test and the Practical Test. Once you have a valid provisional licence you may take the Theory Test at any time, but you must pass it before you are allowed to apply for the Practical Test. The AA publishes a number of different driving books including the official theory questions from the DSA (Driving Standards Agency).

It's important that you should not take your Theory Test too early in your course of practical lessons. This is because you need the experience of meeting real hazards while learning to drive, to help you pass the hazard perception element of the Theory Test.

TAKING THE THEORY TEST

You will have 40 minutes to complete the question part of the test, using a touch-screen. The test is a set of 35 questions drawn from a bank of almost a 1000, all of which have multiple-choice answers. In order to pass the test you must achieve a minimum of 30 correct answers within the given time. The Government may change the pass mark from time to time. Your driving instructor will be able to tell you if there has been a change.

The questions, complete with multiple-choice answers, are presented to you one at a time on a computer screen. You indicate your answer by touching the screen. You can go backwards and forwards through the questions and change the answers at any time. It is easy to use even if you have no prior computer experience.

The test is available in a wide range of languages and can also be listened to

through headphones for those with reading difficulties.

HAZARD PERCEPTION

The aim of Hazard Perception is to find out how good you are at noticing developing hazards coming up on the road ahead. The test will also show how much you know about the risks to you as a driver, risks to your passengers and risks to other road users.

The test lasts about 20 minutes. First you will be given some instructions explaining how the test works; you'll also get a chance to practise with the computer and mouse before you start the test.

Next you will see 14 film or video clips of real street scenes with traffic. The scenes are shot from the point of view of a driver in a car and there are 15 scoreable hazards. As soon as you notice a hazard developing, click on the mouse control. You will have plenty of time to see the hazard – but the sooner you notice it, the more marks you will score. You need to concentrate on the test because unlike the questions section, you won't have an opportunity to go back to an earlier clip and change your response.

You currently have to score 44 out of 75 to pass Hazard Perception but the pass mark may change. Check with your instructor or the Driving Standards Agency (DSA) before sitting your test.

At the end of the test you will be told your scores. You have to pass both hazard perception and the questions to pass your Theory Test, or you will have to take both parts again next time.

LEARNING DRIVING SKILLS

Driving is a skill that has to be learned; there is no such thing as a 'natural' driver. It's true that some people have a greater aptitude for learning driving skills but everyone will benefit from the tuition by a professional driving instructor (ADI).

The most efficient and cost-effective way to learn to drive is to accept that there is no short-cut approach. Agree with your instructor a planned course of tuition suited to your needs, take regular lessons, don't skip weeks and expect to pick up where you left off. Ensure the full official syllabus is covered and, as your skills develop, get as much practice as possible with a relative or friend – but make sure they are legally able to supervise your practice. They must be over 21 years of age and have held a full driving licence for at least three years.

TAKING THE PRACTICAL TEST

Once you have passed your Theory Test, and with your instructor's guidance, you can plan for a suitable test date. Having this goal to look forward to will help to maintain your progress and motivation.

The test is all about making sure that those who pass are competent and safe in the basic skills of driving. During the test you will be expected to drive for

about 40 minutes in various road situations, some of which will be higher speed roads possibly up to the maximum 70mph. You will be asked to perform two out of the three reversing manoeuvres for which you have been trained, and you may or may not be asked to perform an emergency stop.

In order to pass the driving test, you must drive

- without committing any serious fault

  or

- without committing more than 15 driving errors of a less serious nature.

CHANGES TO THE PRACTICAL TEST

From September 2003 you will also be asked to answer two vehicle safety check questions, one 'show me' and one 'tell me'. These questions are to make sure that you know how to check that your vehicle is safe to drive. One or both of the questions answered incorrectly will result in one driving fault being recorded.

Questions fall into three categories

- Identify
- Tell me how you would check
- Show me how you check

Although some checks may require you to identify where fluid levels would be checked, you will not be asked to touch a hot engine or physically check fluid levels. You may refer to vehicle information system (if fitted) when answering questions on fluid levels and tyre pressures.

All vehicles differ slightly so it is important that you get to know all the safety systems and engine layout in the vehicle in which you plan to take your practical test.

Examples of Safety Check Questions

? *Identify where you would check the engine oil and tell me how you would check the oil level.*

? *Identify where is the washer fluid reservoir how you would check the washer fluid level.*

? *Tell me how you would check that the brake lights are working on this car.*

? *Tell me how you would check that the tyres have sufficient tread depth and that their general condition is safe to use on the road.*

? *Show me how you check the horn is working (off road only).*

? *Show me how you check the handbrake for excessive wear.*

Your driving instructor will be trained to teach you about making sure your vehicle is safe for use.

If during learning to drive you have covered the full syllabus with your driving instructor *and* have taken the time to learn and understand the law regarding vehicle safety and maintenance (see *The Highway Code*) you will be adequately equipped to do what is asked.

Those who pass the driving test first time are those who commit themselves to a planned course of tuition, have sufficient lessons and as much practice as possible, and then drive as they have been taught.

MORE INFORMATION

For more practical information on the Theory Test, Hazard Perception and the Practical Test visit www.theAA.com and www.dsa.gov.uk.

FURTHER READING

Available from all good bookshops

AA Theory Test: The Official Questions & Answers (AA Publishing)

AA Theory Test and the Highway Code (AA Publishing)

AA Driving Test Theory Made Easy (AA Publishing)

AA Driving Test Pass First Time (AA Publishing)

Good defensive driving depends on adopting the right attitude from the start. These questions will test your knowledge of what is required before you even sit in the driver's seat.

1 What do you need before you can drive on a public road?

Answer _____

2 The best way to learn is to have regular planned tuition with an ADI (Approved Driving Instructor).

An ADI is someone who has taken and
passed all three driving instructor's

e __ __ __ __ __ __ __ __ __ __ __ and is

on the official r__ __ __ __ __ __ __

Complete the sentence

3 Anyone supervising a learner must be at least __ __ years old and must

have held (and still hold) a full driving licence (motor car) for at least

t__ __ __ __ years

Complete the sentence

4 Your tuition vehicle must display L-plates. Where should they be placed?

Answer _____

> **HINTS & TIPS**
>
> A FULLY QUALIFIED ADI SHOULD DISPLAY A GREEN CERTIFICATE ON THE WINDSCREEN OF THEIR CAR. ASK TO SEE IT.

5 Young and inexperienced drivers are more vulnerable. Is this true or false?

Answer _____

6 Showing responsibility to yourself and others is the key to being a safe driver. Ask yourself, would you ...

	Yes	No
1 Want to drive with someone who has been drinking?	☐	☐
2 Want to drive with someone who takes risks and puts other lives at risk?	☐	☐
3 Want to drive with someone who does not concentrate?	☐	☐
4 Want to drive with someone who drives too fast?	☐	☐

7 Do you want to be a safe and responsible driver?

Tick the correct box

Yes ☐ No ☐

8 You must pass a theory test before you can take the practical test. When would be the best time to sit this test?

Mark two answers

1 Before applying for a provisional licence ☐

2 Just before taking the practical test ☐

3 Some time during the early weeks of your driving lessons ☐

4 After full study of available training materials ☐

ANSWERS ON PAGE 117

SECTION 1

9 To use the controls safely you need to adopt a suitable driving position. There are a number of checks you should make.

Fill in the missing words

1 Check the h _ _ _ _ _ _ _ _ _ is on.

2 Check the d _ _ _ _ are shut.

3 Check your s _ _ _ is in the correct position.

4 Check the h _ _ _ r _ _ _ _ _ _ _ _ _ is adjusted to give maximum protection.

5 Check the driving m _ _ _ _ _ _ are adjusted to give maximum rear view.

6 Check your s _ _ _ b _ _ _ is securely fastened.

10 Here is a list of controls and a list of functions.

Match each function to its control by placing the appropriate letter in the box

THE FUNCTIONS	THE CONTROLS	
A To control the direction in which you want to travel	THE HANDBRAKE	☐
B To slow or stop the vehicle	THE DRIVING MIRRORS	☐
C To increase or decrease the engine's speed	THE GEAR LEVER	☐
D To give you a clear view behind	THE CLUTCH	☐
E To hold the vehicle still when it is stationary	THE STEERING WHEEL	☐
F To enable you to change gear	THE FOOT-BRAKE	☐
G To enable you to make or break contact between the engine and the wheels	THE ACCELERATOR	☐

Fill in the missing word

The accelerator can also be called the g _ _ pedal

ANSWERS ON PAGE 117

11 Which foot should you use for each of these controls (in cars with a manual gearbox)?

R = *Right foot*   L = *Left foot*

The foot-brake ☐   The clutch ☐   The accelerator ☐

12 Are the following statements about steering true or false?

True False

1 I must keep both hands on the wheel at all times. ☐ ☐

2 To keep good control I should feed the wheel through my hands. ☐ ☐

3 I can place my hands at any position as long as I am comfortable. ☐ ☐

4 When going round corners, it is best to cross my hands (hand over hand). ☐ ☐

5 I should never take both hands off the wheel when the vehicle is moving. ☐ ☐

6 To straighten up I should feed the wheel back through my hands. ☐ ☐

13 Match each of the following controls to its function.

THE FUNCTIONS	THE CONTROLS	
A To enable you to see the road ahead and other road users to see you without causing dazzle	THE DIRECTION INDICATORS	☐
B To show other road users which way you intend to turn	DIPPED BEAM	☐
C To use only when visibility is 100metres/yards or less	MAIN BEAM	☐
D To enable you to see further, but not to be used when there is oncoming traffic	REAR FOG LAMP	☐
E To warn other road users of your presence	HORN	☐
F To warn other road users when you are temporarily obstructing traffic	HAZARD LIGHTS	☐

ANSWERS ON PAGE 117

SECTION 2

1 The following is a list of actions involved in moving off from rest. Number the boxes 1 to 9 to show the correct sequence

The first box has been filled in to give you a start

| 1 | **A** Press the clutch down fully

| | **B** Check your mirrors

| | **C** Set the accelerator pedal

| | **D** Move the gear lever into 1st gear

| | **E** Decide whether you need to give a signal

| | **F** Let the clutch come to biting point and hold it steady

| | **G** Check your blind spot

| | **H** If safe, release the handbrake and let the clutch up a little more

| | **I** Press the accelerator pedal a little more and let the clutch up fully

ANSWERS ON PAGE (117)

2 The following is a list of actions required for stopping normally. Number the boxes 1 to 9 to show the correct sequence.

The first box has been filled in to give you a start

| 1 | **A** Check your mirrors

| | **B** Take your foot off the accelerator pedal

| | **C** Decide whether you need to signal and, if necessary, do so

| | **D** Press the brake pedal, lightly at first and then more firmly

| | **E** As the car stops, ease the pressure off the foot-brake (except when you are on a slope)

| | **F** Just before the car stops, press the clutch pedal right down

| | **G** Put the gear lever into neutral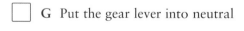

| | **H** Apply the handbrake fully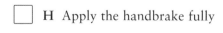

| | **I** Take both feet off the pedals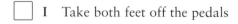

ANSWERS ON PAGE (117)

Gears enable you to select the power you need from the engine to perform a particular task.

3 Which gear gives you the most power?

Answer [ ]

4 If you were travelling at 60mph on a clear road, which gear would you most likely select?

5 When approaching and turning a corner, as shown in the diagram, which gear would you most likely use?

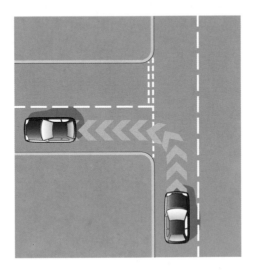

Answer [ ]

ANSWERS ON PAGE 117

6 You need to change gear to match your e__ __ __ __ __ speed to the speed at which your v__ __ __ __ __ __ is travelling. The s__ __ __ __ the engine is making will help you know w__ __ __ to change gear.

Complete the sentences

7 Number the boxes to show the correct sequence of actions required when changing up.

The first box has been filled in for you

| 1 | **A** Place your left hand on the gear lever

| | **B** Move the gear lever to the next highest position

| | **C** Press the clutch pedal down fully and ease off the accelerator pedal

| | **D** Let the clutch pedal come up fully and, at the same time, press the accelerator pedal

| | **E** Put your left hand back on the steering wheel

HINTS & TIPS

IN YOUR DRIVING TEST, YOU WILL BE EXPECTED TO SHOW THAT YOU CAN CONTROL THE CAR SMOOTHLY. IF YOU SHOULD STALL, PUT THE GEARS IN NEUTRAL AND THE HANDBRAKE ON, AND START AGAIN.

ANSWERS ON PAGE 117

8 Are the following statements about changing down true or false?

Tick the appropriate boxes   True False

1 I would stay in the highest gear as long as possible, even if my engine started to labour ☐ ☐

2 I would change down early so that the engine helps to slow the car down ☐ ☐

3 I would avoid using the foot-brake as much as possible ☐ ☐

4 I would usually slow the car down by using the foot-brake first. Then, when I am at the required speed, I would change down to the appropriate gear ☐ ☐

5 I would always change down through the gears so that I do not miss out any intermediate gears ☐ ☐

9 When changing gear, I should look ...

1 Ahead ☐   *2 At the gear lever* ☐   *3 At my feet* ☐

Which is correct?

10 Do's and don'ts   Do Don't

1 Force the gear lever if there is any resistance ☐ ☐

2 Rush the gear changes ☐ ☐

3 Match your speed with the correct gear ☐ ☐

4 Use the brakes, where necessary, to reduce speed before changing down ☐ ☐

5 Listen to the sound of the engine ☐ ☐

6 Take your eyes off the road when changing gear ☐ ☐

7 Hold the gear lever longer than necessary ☐ ☐

8 Coast with the clutch down or the gear lever in neutral ☐ ☐

11   Which wheels turn when you turn the steering wheel?

   A   *The front wheels*   B   *The back wheels*

   Answer

12   When you turn your steering wheel to the right, which way do your wheels turn?

   A   *To the right*   B   *To the left*

   Answer

13   The steering lock is ...

   A   *The locking mechanism that stops the steering wheel from moving when the ignition key is removed*

   B   *The angle through which the wheels turn when the steering wheel is turned*

   Answer

14   Which wheels follow the shorter pathway?

   A   *The front wheels*

   B   *The back wheels*

   Answer

ANSWERS ON PAGE 118

SECTION 2

15 Which is the correct position for normal driving?

Put letter A, B or C in the box   Answer ☐

A   B   C

16 Which diagram shows the correct pathway when driving normally?

Put a letter A or B in the box   Answer ☐

A   B

17 Pushing the clutch pedal down ...

A *Releases the engine from the wheels*

B *Engages the engine with the wheels*   Answer [ ]

18 The point where the clutch plates meet is called the b_ _ _ _ _ point.

Fill in the missing word

19 By controlling the amount of contact between the clutch plates, it is possible to control the speed of the car.

Would you use this control ...

Tick the appropriate boxes   True False

1   *When moving away from rest?*   [ ]   [ ]

2   *When manoeuvring the car in reverse gear?*   [ ]   [ ]

3   *When slowing down to turn a corner?*   [ ]   [ ]

4   *In very slow moving traffic?*   [ ]   [ ]

5   *To slow the car down?*   [ ]   [ ]

HINTS ✔ & TIPS

REMEMBER: MSM STANDS FOR MIRROR, SIGNAL, MANOEUVRE. ALWAYS USE THIS ROUTINE WHEN MOVING OFF, TURNING OR OVERTAKING.

ANSWERS ON PAGE (118)

1 A junction is a point where t __ __ o__ m__ __ __ r__ __ __ __ __ meet.

Complete the sentence

2 Here are five types of junction. Name them

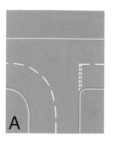

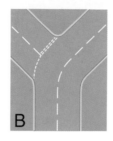

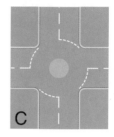

_____   _____   _____

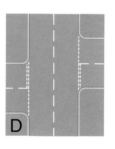

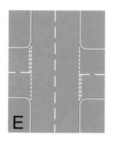

HINTS ✔ & TIPS

AT A STOP SIGN YOU MUST
STOP – BUT YOU NEED
ONLY APPLY THE
HANDBRAKE IF NECESSARY

_____   _____

3 Match these road signs to the junctions shown above.

*Put letters **A**, **B**, **C**, **D** and **E** in the boxes*

1 ☐   2 ☐   3 ☐   4 ☐   5 ☐

4 What do these signs mean?

1 Stop and give way

2 Slow down, look, and proceed if safe

3 Give way to traffic on the major road

Put a number in each box   A ☐   B ☐

5 At every junction you should follow a safe routine.

Put the following into the correct order by numbering the boxes 1 to 5

☐ Signal   ☐ Speed   ☐ Position   ☐ Mirrors   ☐ Look

6 The diagram shows a car turning right into a minor road. The boxes are numbered to show the correct sequence of actions.

Complete the sentence

At point 5 you should look and

a _ _ _ _ _ the situation,

d _ _ _ _ _ to go or wait,

and a _ _ accordingly.

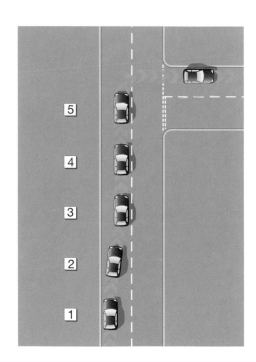

ANSWERS ON PAGE ⑴⑴⑻

7 Turning left into a minor road.

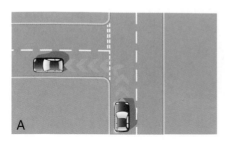 

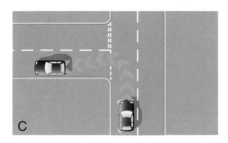 

Which diagram shows the best path to follow when driving a motor car A, B, C or D?

Answer ☐

8 You turn into a side road. Pedestrians are already crossing it. Should you ...

Tick the appropriate box

☐ A Sound your horn ☐ B Slow down and give way

☐ C Flash your lights ☐ D Wave them across

ANSWERS ON PAGE ⓘ118

9 Turning right into a minor road.

Which diagram shows the best path to follow: A, B, C or D?   Answer

A

B

C

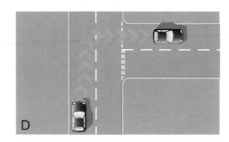

D

10 These are the golden rules for emerging from junctions.

Complete the sentences

1   Always use your m_ _ _ _ _ _ to check the speed and

p _ _ _ _ _ _ _ _ of vehicles behind.

2   Always cancel your s_ _ _ _ _ _ .

3   Speed up to a s_ _ _ speed after joining the new road.

4   Keep a s_ _ _ d_ _ _ _ _ _ _ _ between you and the
vehicle ahead.

5   Do not attempt to o_ _ _ _ _ _ _ _ until you can assess
the new road.

ANSWERS ON PAGE (118)

SECTION 3

11 **All crossroads must be approached with caution.**

Match Actions 1, 2 and 3 listed below with these diagrams

ACTIONS

1 Approach with caution, look well ahead and be prepared to stop. Remember other drivers may assume they have priority.

2 Look well ahead, slow down and be prepared to give way to traffic on the major road.

3 Look well ahead and into the side roads for approaching vehicles. Remember other drivers may not give you priority.

Answer ☐ Answer ☐ Answer ☐

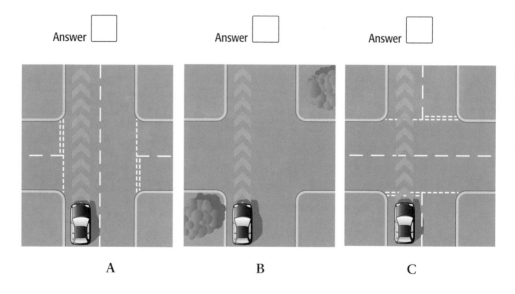

A B C

ANSWERS ON PAGE (118)

HINTS ✔ & TIPS

AT AN UNMARKED CROSSROADS, NO ONE HAS PRIORITY. BE EXTRA-CAUTIOUS AT THESE JUNCTIONS.

12 **Which of the following statements describes the correct procedure when approaching a roundabout?**

*Put letter **A**, **B** or **C** in the box*

A The broken white line at a roundabout means I must stop and give way to traffic already on the roundabout.

B The broken white line at a roundabout means I must give priority to traffic already on the roundabout.

C The broken white line means I should give way to any traffic approaching pfrom my immediate right.

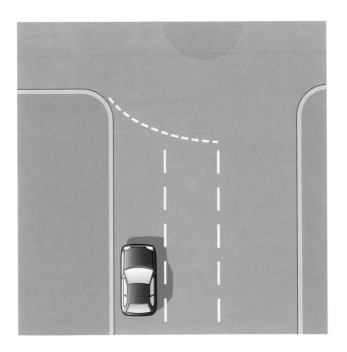

Answer ☐

ANSWERS ON PAGE ⑱

13 The following sentences give guidance on lane discipline on a roundabout.

Fill in the missing words

1 When turning left at a roundabout, I should stay in the _ _ _ _ hand lane and should stay in that lane throughout.

2 When going ahead at a roundabout, I should be in the _ _ _ _ hand land, and should stay in that lane throughout, unless conditions dictate otherwise.

3 When turning right at a roundabout, I should approach in the r_ _ _ _ hand lane, or approach as if turning right at a junction, and stay in that lane throughout.

14 The letters A, B and C in the diagram mark places where you should signal.

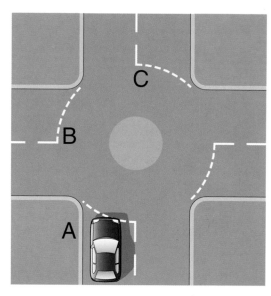

ANSWERS ON PAGE (118)

Complete the sentences

1 I would signal at A when turning _ _ _ _.

2 I would signal at B when g_ _ _ _ _ _ _ _ _ _.

3 I would signal at A and at C when turning _ _ _ _ _ _.

15 At a roundabout you should always use a safe routine.

Fill in the missing words

m__ __ __ __ __ __ __, s __ __ __ __ __, p__ __ __ __ __ __ __,

s__ __ __ __, l__ __ __.

16 What does this sign mean?

1 Roundabout

2 Mini-roundabout

3 Vehicles may pass either side.

Write 1, 2 or 3 in the box

Answer ☐

HINTS ✔ & TIPS

BE CAREFUL AT ROUNDABOUTS WHERE
DESTINATIONS ARE MARKED FOR EACH LANE.
MAKE SURE YOU ARE IN THE CORRECT LANE
FOR YOUR DESTINATION.

ANSWERS ON PAGE 119

SECTION 4

1 It is safest to park off the road or in a car park whenever possible. If you have to park on the road, think ...

Fill in the missing words

1 Is it s_ _ _ ?

2 Is it c_ _ _ _ _ _ _ _ _ _ _?

3 Is it l_ _ _ _ ?

ANSWERS ON PAGE 119

2 In this diagram four of the cars are parked illegally or without consideration of others.

Put the numbers of these cars in the boxes ☐ ☐ ☐ ☐

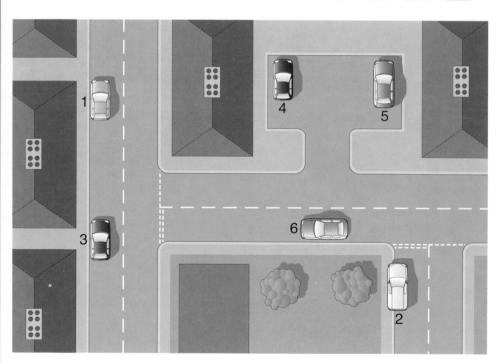

For reverse parallel parking manoeuvres, see pages 54–7.

3 Check how well you know the rules about where you may and may not park.

Are the following statements true or false?

True False

1 In a narrow street, I should park with two wheels up on the pavement to leave more room for other traffic. ☐ ☐

2 I am allowed to park in a 'Disabled' space if all other spaces are full. ☐ ☐

3 I should not park on the zig-zag lines near a zebra crossing. ☐ ☐

4 Red lines painted on the road mean 'No Stopping'. ☐ ☐

Tick the correct boxes

4 List three places not mentioned in Question 3 where you should *not* park.

1 _____

_____

2 _____

_____

3 _____

_____

HINTS ✔ & TIPS

USE YOUR *HIGHWAY CODE* TO FIND OUT MORE ABOUT PARKING REGULATIONS

ANSWERS ON PAGE ⓵⁹

1 The diagram shows a stationary vehicle on the left-hand side of the road.

Which should have priority, vehicle 1 or vehicle 2?

Answer

ANSWERS ON PAGE 119

2 This diagram shows a steep downward hill with an obstruction on the right-hand side of the road. Which vehicle should be given priority, vehicle 1 or vehicle 2?

Answer

3 The diagram shows two vehicles, travelling in opposite
directions, turning right at a crossroads.

Are these statements true or false? Tick the appropriate boxes

True False

1 The safest route is to pass each other offside
to offside. ☐ ☐

2 If the approaching vehicle flashes its headlamps, I should
turn as quickly as possible. ☐ ☐

3 I should always try to get eye-to-eye contact with the
driver of the other vehicle to determine which course
to take. ☐ ☐

SECTION 5

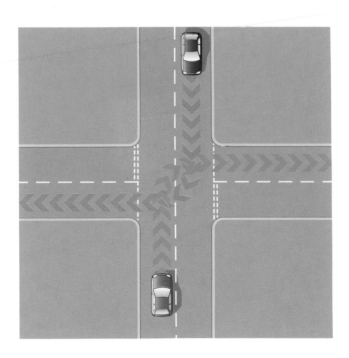

ANSWERS ON PAGE 119

SECTION 5

4 Which of the following factors, illustrated in the diagram, should be taken into consideration when turning right into a side road?

Tick the appropriate boxes

	Yes	No
1 The speed of the approaching vehicle (A)	☐	☐
2 The roadworks	☐	☐
3 The speed of vehicle B	☐	☐
4 The cyclist	☐	☐
5 Your speed (vehicle C)	☐	☐
6 The pedestrians	☐	☐
7 The car waiting to turn right (D)	☐	☐

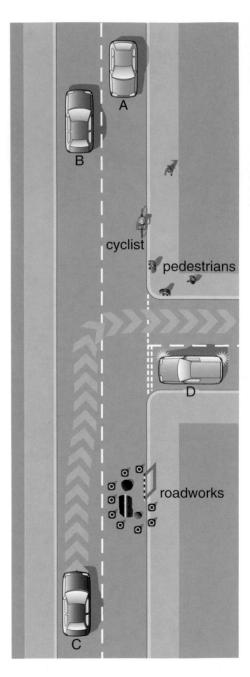

HINTS & TIPS

CYCLISTS ARE VULNERABLE ROAD USERS, SO YOU SHOULD TAKE SPECIAL CARE. PEDESTRIANS HAVE PRIORITY IF THEY HAVE ALREADY STEPPED INTO THE SIDE ROAD.

ANSWERS ON PAGE 119

1 Are the following statements true or false when stopping in
an emergency?

Tick the correct boxes   True False

1 Stopping in an emergency increases the risk of skidding. ☐ ☐

2 I should push the brake pedal down harder as I
slow down. ☐ ☐

3 It is important to react quickly. ☐ ☐

4 I should always remember to look in my mirrors as
I slow down. ☐ ☐

5 I should signal left to tell other road users what I am doing. ☐ ☐

6 I should keep both hands on the wheel. ☐ ☐

7 I should always check my mirrors and look round before
moving off. ☐ ☐

2 Is the following statement true or false?

An emergency stop will be carried out on every driving test

Tick the correct box   True False

☐ ☐

> **HINTS ✔ & TIPS**
>
> ALWAYS KEEP A SAFE DISTANCE
> BETWEEN YOUR VEHICLE AND THE
> ONE IN FRONT, SO THAT YOU
> WOULD BE ABLE TO STOP SAFELY IN
> AN EMERGENCY

ANSWERS ON PAGE 119

SECTION 6

3 Cadence braking is a technique which can be used in very slippery conditions in an emergency.

Fill in the missing words

The technique requires you to p__ __ __ the brake pedal. The procedure to follow is:

1 Apply m__ __ __ __ __ __ pressure.

2 Release the brake pedal just as the wheels are about to l__ __ __.

3 Then q__ __ __ __ __ __ apply the brakes again. Apply and release the brakes until the vehicle has stopped. This technique should only be used in emergency situations.

4 Anti-lock braking systems (ABS)* work in a similar way to cadence braking.

Fill in the missing words

When braking in an emergency, ABS brakes allow you to s__ __ __ __ and b__ __ __ __ at the same time. You do not have to p__ __ __ the brakes as you would in cadence braking. When using ABS you keep the p__ __ __ __ __ __ __ applied.

Are these statements about ABS braking true or false?

Tick the correct boxes

1 Cars fitted with ABS braking cannot skid. ☐

2 I do not need to leave as much room between me and the car in front if I have ABS brakes because I know I can stop in a shorter distance. ☐

*ABS is a registered trade mark of Bosch (Germany). ABS stands for Anti-Blockiersystem

ANSWERS ON PAGE (119)

The distance taken for a car to reach stopping point divides into thinking distance and braking distance.

5 Could these factors affect thinking distance?

Tick the appropriate boxes

Yes No

1 The condition of your tyres ☐ ☐

2 Feeling tired or unwell ☐ ☐

3 Speed of reaction ☐ ☐

4 Going downhill ☐ ☐

6 Most drivers' reaction time is well over ...

Tick the appropriate box

½ second ☐

1 second ☐

5 seconds ☐

7 Stopping distance depends partly on the speed at which the car is travelling.

Complete the sentences

1 At 30mph your overall stopping distance will be __ __ metres or __ __ feet.

2 At 50mph your thinking distance will be _ . __ metres or __ __ feet.

3 At 70mph your overall stopping distance will be __ __ metres or __ __ __feet.

ANSWERS ON PAGE (119)

8 Stopping distance also varies according to road conditions.

Complete the sentences

In wet weather your vehicle will take l __ __ __ __ __ to stop. You should therefore allow m __ __ __ time.

HINTS ✓ & TIPS

YOU NEED TO **DOUBLE** YOUR NORMAL STOPPING DISTANCE IN WET WEATHER – AND MULTIPLY BY AS MUCH AS **10** WHEN CONDITIONS ARE ICY.

9 Too many accidents are caused by drivers driving too close to the vehicle in front. A safe gap between you and the vehicle in front can be measured by noting a stationary object and counting in seconds the time that lapses between the vehicle in front passing that object and your own vehicle passing that object.

Complete the sentence

Only a fool b __ __ __ __ __ the t __ __ s __ __ __ __ __ __ rule.

HINTS ✓ & TIPS

IF A VEHICLE IS TRAVELLING TOO CLOSE BEHIND YOU, THEN INCREASE THE GAP YOU HAVE AHEAD. ALWAYS THINK FOR THE DRIVER BEHIND.

ANSWERS ON PAGE 120

1 **Are these statements about moving off at an angle true or false?**

Tick the correct boxes   True False

1   I should check my mirrors
    as I am pulling out.   ☐   ☐

2   I should check my mirrors
    and blindspot before
    I pull out.   ☐   ☐

3   I should move out as
    quickly as possible.   ☐   ☐

4   The amount of steering
    required will depend
    on how close I am to
    the vehicle in front.   ☐   ☐

5   I should look for
    oncoming traffic.   ☐   ☐

6   As long as I am
    signalling, people will
    know what I am doing.
    I will be able to pull
    out because somebody
    will let me in.   ☐   ☐

ANSWERS ON PAGE 120

2   Are these statements about moving off uphill true or false?

Tick the correct boxes   True   False

1   On an uphill gradient the
car will tend to roll back.   ☐ ☐

2   To stop the car rolling
back I need to use more
acceleration.   ☐ ☐

3   I do not need to use
the handbrake.   ☐ ☐

4   The biting point may be
slightly higher.   ☐ ☐

5   I need to press the
accelerator pedal
further down than
when moving off
on the level.   ☐ ☐

6   I need to allow more
time to pull away.   ☐ ☐

7   The main controls
I use will be the clutch
pedal, the accelerator
pedal and the
handbrake.   ☐ ☐

ANSWERS ON PAGE 120

3   **Are these statements about moving off downhill true or false?**

Tick the correct boxes

True False

1 The car will tend to roll forwards. ☐ ☐

2 The main controls I use will be the handbrake, the clutch pedal and the accelerator pedal. ☐ ☐

3 The only gear I can move off in is 1st gear. ☐ ☐

4 I should release the handbrake while keeping the foot-brake applied. ☐ ☐

5 I should look round just before moving off. ☐ ☐

6 I must not have my foot on the foot-brake as I start to release the clutch. ☐ ☐

4 The following statements are about approaching a junction when going uphill or downhill. With which do you agree?

When going downhill ...

Yes No

1 It is more difficult to slow down ☐ ☐

2 Putting the clutch down will help slow the car down ☐ ☐

3 The higher the gear, the greater the control ☐ ☐

4 When changing gear you may need to use the foot-brake at the same time as the clutch ☐ ☐

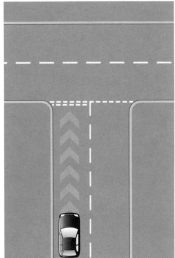

When going uphill ...

5 Early use of mirrors, signals, brakes, gears and steering will help to position the car correctly

Yes No

☐ ☐

6 You may need to use your handbrake more often ☐ ☐

7 When you change gear, the car tends to slow down ☐ ☐

ANSWERS ON PAGE (120)

1 **Before reversing there are three things to consider.**

Fill in the missing words

1   Is it s__ __ __?

2   Is it c__ __ __ __ __ __ __ __ __?

3   Is it within the l__ __?

2 **Are the following statements about reversing true or false?**

Tick the appropriate boxes

		True	False
1	Other road users should see what I am doing and wait for me.	☐	☐
2	I should wave pedestrians on, so that I can get on with the manoeuvre more quickly.	☐	☐
3	I should avoid being too hesitant.	☐	☐
4	I should avoid making other road users slow down or change course.	☐	☐

3 **How should you hold the steering wheel when reversing left?**

Answer ☐

A   B   C   *Which is correct?*

ANSWERS ON PAGE **120**

4 These statements are all about reversing.

Tick those which you think are correct

True False

1 My car will respond differently in reverse gear. ☐ ☐

2 My car will feel no different. ☐ ☐

3 Steering is not affected. The car responds the same as when going forward. ☐ ☐

4 The steering will feel different. I will have to wait for the steering to take effect. ☐ ☐

5 Which way will the rear of the car go when it is reversed? Left or right?

Car A

Car B

Answer

Answer

_____

_____

ANSWERS ON PAGE ⟨120⟩

SECTION 8

6 It is important to move the vehicle slowly when reversing.

Complete the sentence

Moving the vehicle slowly is safer because I have control and it allows me to carry out good o__ __ __ __ __ __ __ __ __ __ checks.

7 When reversing, good observation is vital. Where should you look?

Tick the correct answer

1	At the kerb ☐	2	Ahead ☐
3	Where your car is going ☐	4	Out of the back window ☐

8 Are these statements about reversing round a corner true or false?

Tick the correct boxes   True False

1 If the corner is sharp, I need to be further away from the kerb.   ☐ ☐

2 The distance from the kerb makes no difference.   ☐ ☐

3 I should try to stay reasonably close to the kerb all the way round.   ☐ ☐

9 Before reversing I should check ...

Tick the correct box

1	Behind me ☐	2	Ahead and to the rear ☐
3	My door mirrors ☐	4	All round ☐

ANSWERS ON PAGE (120)

10 Which position is the correct one in which to start steering?

A, B, C or D?   Answer ☐

11 Which way should you steer?

Answer

_____

12 What will happen to the front of the car?

Answer

_____

13 Are these statements about steering when reversing round a corner true or false?

Tick the correct boxes

		True	False
1	The more gradual the corner, the less I have to steer.	☐	☐
2	I need to steer the same for every corner.	☐	☐
3	The sharper the corner, the more I have to steer.	☐	☐

ANSWERS ON PAGE (120)

14 As I enter the new road, I should continue to keep a look-out for

p_ _ _ _ _ _ _ _ _ _ _ and other r_ _ _ u_ _ _ _.

I should s_ _ _ if necessary.

Complete the sentences

ANSWERS ON PAGE 120

15 True or false? When reversing from a major road into a side road on the right, I have to move to the wrong side of the road.

Tick the correct box

True False
☐ ☐

16 Which diagram shows the correct path to follow when moving to the right-hand side of the road? A or B?

Answer ☐

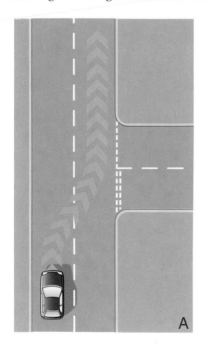

SECTION 8

17 **Which of the following correctly describes your sitting position for reversing to the right?**

1 I will need to sit so that I can see over my right shoulder.

2 I will need to sit so that I can see over my right shoulder, ahead and to the left.

3 My position is the same as when reversing to the left.

Which statement is correct? 1, 2 or 3 Answer ☐

18 **True or false? I may need to change my hand position on the wheel.**

Tick the correct box True ☐ False ☐

19 **True or false? It is easier to judge my position from the kerb when reversing to the right than when reversing to the left.**

Tick the correct box True ☐ False ☐

20 **Reversing to the right is more dangerous than reversing to the left because ...**

1 I cannot see as well

2 I am on the wrong side of the road

3 I might get in the way of vehicles emerging from the side road

Which statement is correct – 1, 2 or 3? Answer ☐

ANSWERS ON PAGE ⓘ121

21 How far down the side road would you reverse before moving over to the left-hand side?

Which diagram is correct? **A** *or* **B?**   Answer ▢

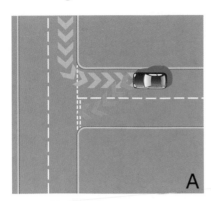 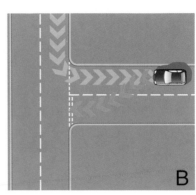

22 Look at the diagrams and decide which is safer.   Answer ▢

A Reversing into a side road   **B** Turning round in the road

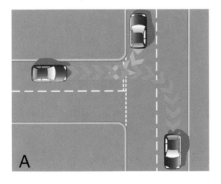 

23 The secret of turning in the road is to move the vehicle s__ __ __ __ __

and steer b__ __ __ __ __ __.

Complete the sentence   ANSWERS ON PAGE ⑫⑪

24 I must be able to complete the manoeuvre in three moves:

1 forward, 2 reverse, 3 forward.

True or false?

Tick the correct box

True False

□ □

25 Before manoeuvring what should you take into consideration?

Tick the correct boxes

1 The size of your engine □

2 The width of the road □

3 The road camber □

4 The steering circle of your vehicle □

5 Parking restrictions □

HINTS & TIPS

WHEN TAKING YOUR TEST, YOU WILL BE ASSESSED ON HOW WELL YOU CAN CONTROL THE CAR; SO DON'T RUSH YOUR MANOEUVRES.

26 Before moving forward, it is important to check a_ _ r_ _ _ _ for other road users.

Complete the sentence

ANSWERS ON PAGE 121

27 **Turning in the road requires proper use of the steering wheel.**

Answer the following questions

1 When going forwards, which way should you steer?

Answer _____

2 Before you reach the kerb ahead, what should you do?

Answer _____

3 When reversing, which way should you steer?

Answer _____

4 Before you reach the kerb behind you, what should you do?

Answer _____

5 As you move forward again, which way should you steer to straighten up?

Answer _____

SECTION 8

ANSWERS ON PAGE 121

28 **Reversing is a potentially dangerous manoeuvre. Good observation is essential.**

Answer the following questions

1 If you are steering left when reversing, which shoulder should you look over?

Answer _____

2 As you begin to steer to the right, where should you look?

Answer _____

HINTS ✔ & TIPS

IN YOUR DRIVING TEST YOU MAY
BE ASKED TO REVERSE INTO A
PARKING BAY AT THE TEST
CENTRE, OR TO PARK BEHIND
ANOTHER CAR, USING REVERSE
GEAR. SO MAKE SURE YOU
PRACTISE THESE MANOEUVRES.

29 **When parking between two cars ...**

1 The car is more manoeuvrable when driving forwards

2 The car is more manoeuvrable when reversing

3 There is no difference between going into the space forwards or reversing into it

Which statement is correct? 1, 2 or 3?

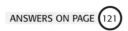

ANSWERS ON PAGE (121)

30 The diagram shows a car preparing to reverse into a parking space. Which position is the correct one in which to start steering left?

Answer ☐

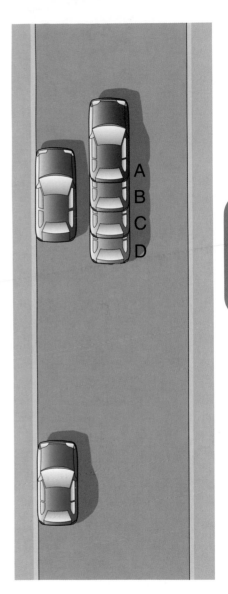

31 With practice you should be able to park in a gap ...

1 Your own car length

2 1½ times your own car length

3 2 times your own car length

4 2½ times your own car length

Answer ☐

ANSWERS ON PAGE 121

32 Use the diagram to help you answer the following questions.

1 Which way would you steer?

Answer _____

2 At this point what would you try to line up with the offside (right-hand side) of your vehicle?

Answer _____

3 As you straighten up what do you have to be careful of?

Answer _____

4 What do you need to do to straighten up?

Answer _____

5 What would you need to do in order to position the vehicle parallel to the kerb?

Answer _____

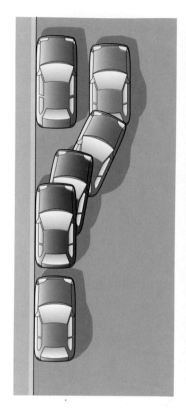

33 True or false? During my driving test ...

Tick the correct boxes

	True	False
1 I will certainly be asked to perform this manoeuvre	☐	☐
2 I have to be able to park in a tight space between two cars	☐	☐
3 It may be that only the lead car is present	☐	☐

ANSWERS ON PAGE (121)

34 When carrying out this manoeuvre, where is it important to look?

Answer _____

35 Look at the diagram and answer the following question.

Which bay should you use and why?

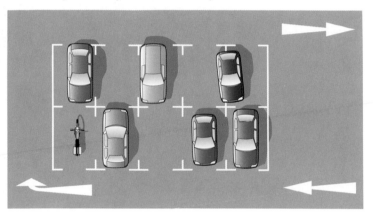

36 Why, wherever possible, should you choose to reverse into a parking bay?

Answer _____

37 As well as being very aware of how c__ __ __ __ I am to the parked cars

on either side, I should also be alert for cars moving near me from all

d__ __ __ __ __ __ __ __ __ __, as well as the possibility of

p__ __ __ __ __ __ __ __ __ __ walking around my car.

Complete the sentence

ANSWERS ON PAGE (121)

1   Traffic lights have three lights, red, amber, and green, which change from one to the other in a set order. Number the boxes 1 to 5 to show the correct order. The first one has been filled in to give you a start.

Amber ☐   Red 1   Red and amber ☐   Red ☐   Green ☐

2   **What do the colours mean?**

Fill in the correct colour for each of the following

1   Go ahead if the way is clear.   Colour _____

2   Stop and wait.   Colour _____

3   Stop unless you have crossed the stop line
    or you are so close to it that stopping
    might cause an accident.   Colour _____

4   Stop and wait at the stop line.   Colour _____

3   **Which of the following statements are true? Tick the appropriate boxes**

On approach to traffic lights you should ...

1   Speed up to get through before they change   ☐

2   Be ready to stop   ☐

3   Look for pedestrians   ☐

4   Sound your horn to urge pedestrians to cross quickly   ☐

SECTION 9

ANSWERS ON PAGE 121

4 Some traffic lights have green filters. Do they mean ...

1 You can filter in the direction of the arrow only when the main light is showing green?

2 You can filter even when the main light is not showing green?

Answer [ ]

5 The diagram shows the three lanes at a set of traffic lights.

Which lane would you use for ...

1 Going ahead   Answer _____

2 Turning right   Answer _____

3 Turning left   Answer _____

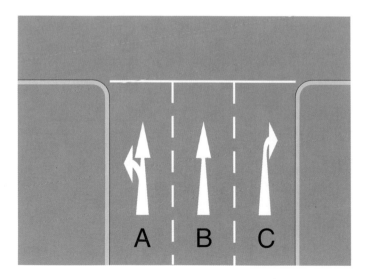

ANSWERS ON PAGE 121

6 At some traffic lights and junctions you will see yellow criss-cross lines (box junctions). Can you ...

Tick the correct boxes

Yes No

1 Wait within them when going ahead if your exit is not clear? ☐ ☐

2 Wait within them when going right if your exit is not clear? ☐ ☐

3 Wait within them if there is oncoming traffic stopping you turning right but your exit is clear? ☐ ☐

Pedestrians have certain rights of way at pedestrian crossings.

7 On approaching a zebra crossing, drivers will notice four features.

Name them

1 _____

2 _____

3 _____

4 _____

ANSWERS ON PAGE (121)

8 **Are these statements about pedestrian crossings true or false?**   True False

1   I cannot park or wait on the zig-zag lines on the approach
    to a zebra crossing.

2   I cannot park or wait on the zig-zag lines on either side of
    the crossing.

3   I can overtake on the zig-zag lines on the approach to a
    crossing as long as the other vehicle is travelling slowly.

4   I must give way to a pedestrian once he/she has stepped on
    to the crossing.

5   If, on approach to a crossing, I intend to slow down or stop,
    I should use a slowing-down arm signal.

Tick the correct boxes

9 **On approaching a pelican crossing, drivers will notice three key features.**

Name them

1   _____

2   _____

3   _____

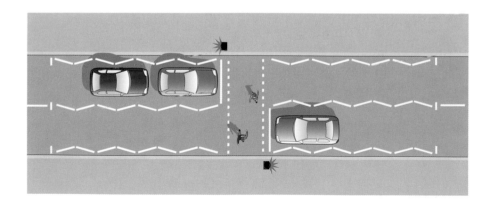

10 If you see a pedestrian at a zebra crossing or pelican crossing carrying a white stick, do you think ...

Tick the correct box

1 He/she has difficulty walking? ☐

2 He/she is visually handicapped? ☐

11 The traffic lights at a pelican crossing have the same meaning as ordinary traffic lights, but they do not have a red and amber phase.

1 What do they show instead of the red and amber phase?

Answer _____

2 What does the light mean?

Answer _____

12 What sound is usually heard at a pelican crossing when the green man is shown to pedestrians?

Answer _____

13 Toucan and puffin crossings are similar to pelican crossings but with one main difference. Name it.

Answer _____

ANSWERS ON PAGE ⟨122⟩

SECTION 9

14 As well as pedestrians, what other type of road users should you watch for at a toucan crossing?

Answer _____

A level crossing is where the road crosses at a railway line. It is potentially dangerous and should be approached with caution.

15 Match each traffic sign below with its correct meaning.

A   B   C    D

1   Level crossing without gates or barriers ☐

2   Level crossing with lights ☐

3   Level crossing with gates or barriers ☐

4   Level crossing without lights ☐

ANSWERS ON PAGE ⓵²²

16 If you break down on a level crossing, should you ...

1   Tell your passengers to wait in the vehicle while you go to get help? ☐

2   Get everybody out and clear of the crossing? ☐

3   Telephone the police? ☐

4   Telephone the signal operator? ☐

5   If there is still time, push your car clear of the crossing? ☐

Tick the appropriate boxes

One-way systems are where all traffic flows in the same direction.

1 Which of these signs means one-way traffic?

A

B

2 Are these statements about one-way systems true or false?

	True	False
1 In one-way streets traffic can pass me on both sides.	☐	☐
2 Roundabouts are one-way systems.	☐	☐
3 For normal driving I should stay on the left.	☐	☐
4 I should look out for road markings and get in lane early.	☐	☐

Tick the correct boxes

As a rule, the more paint on the road, the more important the message.

3 Road markings are divided into three categories.

Fill in the missing words

1 Those which give i__ __ __ __ __ __ __ __ __ __.

2 Those which give w__ __ __ __ __ __ __.

3 Those which give o__ __ __ __ __.

ANSWERS ON PAGE (122)

SECTION 10

4 There are two main advantages which road markings have over other traffic signs. Name them

1 _____

2 _____

5 What do these lines across the road mean?

1 Stop and give way

2 Give priority to traffic coming from the immediate right.

3 Give way to traffic coming from the right.

Answer

A

1 Give way to traffic on the major road.

2 Stop at the line and give way to traffic on the major road.

Answer

B

SECTION 10

ANSWERS ON PAGE 122

6 Where you see double solid white lines painted along the centre of the road, what does this mean?

1 I must not park or wait on the carriageway. ☐

2 I can park between 7pm and 7am. ☐

3 I must not overtake. ☐

4 I must not cross the white line except to turn right or in circumstances beyond my control. ☐

More than one answer may be correct.
Tick any boxes you think are appropriate.

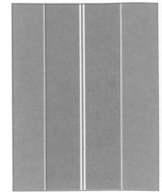

7 What is the purpose of these hatched markings (chevrons)?

Answer _____

_____

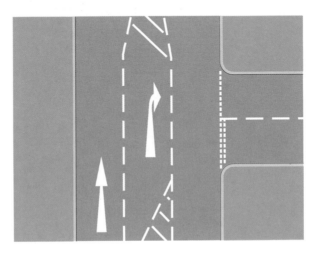

ANSWERS ON PAGE 122

SECTION 10

8 What does it mean if the chevrons are edged with a solid white line?

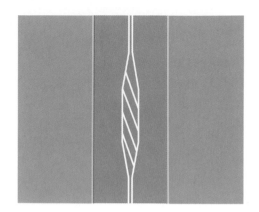

Answer _____

_____

_____

The shape and colour of a sign will help you understand what it means.

9 Look at the sign shapes below and say whether each gives an order, a warning or information.

1

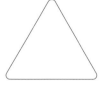

2

3

_____   _____   _____

Answer   *Answer*   *Answer*

10 1 A circular sign with a blue background tells you what

you m__ __ __ do.

2 A circular sign with a red border tells you what you

m__ __ __ n__ __ do.

Complete the sentences

ANSWERS ON PAGE (122)

11 What do these signs mean?

1 *Answer*

_____

_____

_____

2 *Answer*

_____

_____

_____

12 Some junctions have a stop sign, others have a give way sign.

Complete the sentence

A stop sign is usually placed at a junction where

v_ _ _ _ _ is l_ _ _ _ _ _.

ANSWERS ON PAGE 122

13 Information signs are colour-coded.

Match each of the following signs to its colouring.

A White letters on a brown background   MOTORWAY SIGNS ☐

B Black letters on a white background   PRIMARY ROUTES ☐

C Black letters on a white background with a blue border   OTHER ROUTES ☐

D White letters on a blue background with a white border   LOCAL PLACES ☐

E White letters on a green background, yellow route numbers with a white border   TOURIST SIGNS ☐

1 **Good observation is vital in today's busy traffic.**

Complete the sentence

When using my mirrors I should try to make a mental note of the

s_ _ _ _, b_ _ _ _ _ _ _ _ _ and i_ _ _ _ _ _ _ _ _ of

the driver behind.

2 **Driving in built-up areas is potentially dangerous.** ANSWERS ON PAGE 123

Look at this diagram

1 What action should the
driver of car A take?
List four options

A _____

B _____

C _____

D _____

2 What action should the
driver of car B take?
List four options

A _____

B _____

C _____

D _____

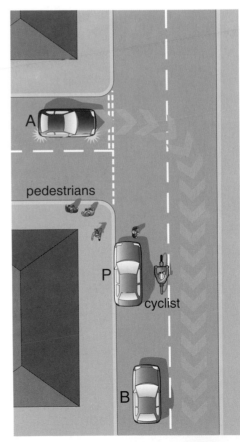

pedestrians

P

cyclist

A

B

SECTION 11

3 Motorcyclists are often less visible than other road users.

Complete this well-known phrase

Think once, think twice, think b__ __ __. ANSWERS ON PAGE (123)

4 When you observe traffic following too close behind you, would you

Tick the correct box

1 Speed up to create a bigger gap? ☐

2 Touch your brake lights to warn the
following driver? ☐

3 Keep to a safe speed, and keep checking
the behaviour and intentions of the
following driver? ☐

> **HINTS ✔ & TIPS**
>
> OBSERVATION MEANS LOOKING ALL AROUND AND SEEING ANYTHING THAT MATTERS. DON'T STARE AT JUST ONE THING – KEEP YOUR EYES MOVING.

5 Some hazards are potential, others are actual and there all the time, such as a bend in the road.

A Name five more actual hazards

1 _____

2 _____

3 _____

4 _____

5 _____

B Name five potential hazards, such as a dog off its lead

1 _____

2 _____

3 _____

4 _____

5 _____

SECTION 11

6 Modern driving requires full concentration.

Are the following statements true or false?

True False

1 Carrying a mobile phone can reduce the stress of a long journey. ☐☐

2 I must not use a hand-held phone while driving. ☐☐

3 Conversation on a hands-free phone can still distract my attention. ☐☐

4 I should pull up in a safe place to make or receive calls. ☐☐

7 When driving, all the following actions have something in common.

Reading a map   *Answer* _____

Eating   _____

Changing a cassette   _____

Listening to loud music   _____

What is it?

ANSWERS ON PAGE 123

SECTION 11

One of the features of driving on the open road is taking bends properly.

8 As a rule you should be travelling at the correct s_ _ _ _, using the correct g_ _ _, and be in the correct p_ _ _ _ _ _ _ _.

9 Should you brake ...

1 Before you enter the bend? ☐

2 As you enter the bend? ☐

3 While negotiating the bend? ☐

Tick the appropriate box

10 Which way does force push a car on a bend?

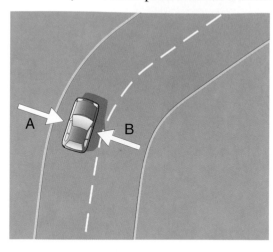

A Inwards

or

B Outwards

Answer ☐

ANSWERS ON PAGE (123)

11 What happens to the weight of the car when you use the brakes?

A It is thrown forwards   **B** It remains even   **C** It is thrown back

Answer ☐

12 When you approach a bend, what position should you be in?

A On a right-hand bend
I should keep to the

_____

B On a left-hand bend
I should keep to the

_____

Complete the sentences

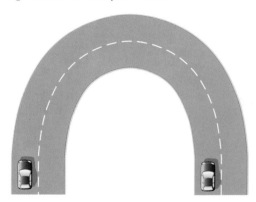

SECTION 11

Overtaking is a potentially dangerous manoeuvre.

13 Before overtaking, consider whether it is really n__ __ __ __ __ __ __ __.

Fill in the missing word

Always use the safety routine when overtaking.

Put these actions into their correct sequence by putting numbers 1 to 7, as seen in the diagram, in the boxes

☐ Signal ☐ Mirrors ☐ Look ☐ Position

☐ Mirrors ☐ Speed ☐ Manoeuvre

14 What is the minimum amount of clearance you should give a cyclist or motor cyclist?

Answer _____

ANSWERS ON PAGE 123

15 There are four situations in which you may, with caution, overtake on the left-hand side of the car in front.

Name them

1 _____

2 _____

3 _____

4 _____

16 List four places where it would be dangerous to overtake.

1 _____

2 _____

3 _____

4 _____

17 Dual carriageways can appear similar to motorways, but there are important differences.

Which of the following statements apply to dual carriageways?

Tick the relevant boxes

1 Reflective studs are not used. ☐

2 Cyclists are allowed. ☐

3 The speed limit is always 60mph. ☐

4 You cannot turn right to enter or leave a dual carriageway. ☐

5 Milk floats and slow moving farm vehicles are prohibited. ☐

ANSWERS ON PAGE (123)

SECTION 11

18 When turning right from a minor road on to a dual carriageway, where would you wait ...

A When there is a wide central reserve?

Answer _____

B When the central reserve is too narrow for your car?

Answer _____

19 When travelling at 70mph on a dual carriageway, which lane would you use?

Answer _____

20 What do these signs mean?

A

Answer

_____

B

Answer

_____

C

Answer

_____

ANSWERS ON PAGE 124

21 Which of the signs in Question 20 (see previous page) would you expect to see on a dual carriageway?

Answer _____

22 Why is it important to plan your movements especially early when leaving a dual carriageway to the right?

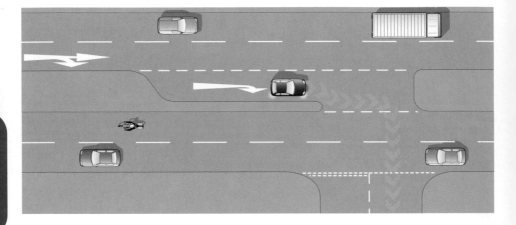

Answer _____

_____

_____

ANSWERS ON PAGE 124

SECTION 11

1 Cars fitted with automatic transmission select the gear depending on the road speed and the load on the engine. They therefore have no c_ _ _ _ _ pedal.

Fill in the missing word

2 The advantages of an automatic car are ...

1 _____

2 _____

3 The gear selector has the same function as a manual selector, but what function do each of the following have?

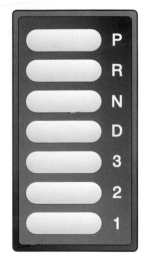

Park _____

Reverse _____

Neutral _____

Drive _____

3rd _____

2nd _____

1st _____

ANSWERS ON PAGE 124

4 **Automatic cars have a device called a kickdown. Is its function ...**

1   To select a higher gear?

2   To select a lower gear manually?

3   To provide quick accelerations when needed?

Tick the correct box

5 **When driving an automatic car, would you select a lower gear ...**   True   False

1   To control speed when going down a steep hill?

2   To slow the car down in normal driving?

3   When going uphill?

4   To overtake, in certain circumstances?

5   When manoeuvring?

6   Before stopping?

Tick the correct boxes

6 **An automatic car has two foot pedals, the foot-brake and the accelerator.**
For normal driving, which foot would you use ...

1   For the brake?   *Answer* _____

2   For the accelerator?   *Answer* _____

ANSWERS ON PAGE (124)

SECTION 12

7 When you are driving an automatic car, using one foot to control both pedals is preferable to using both the left and the right foot. Why?

Answer _____

_____

_____

8 Some cars with automatic transmission have a tendency to 'creep'.

Which gears allow the car to creep?

Answer _____

_____

_____

9 When driving an automatic car, would you use the handbrake ...

1 More than in a manual car?

2 The same?

3 Less?

Tick the correct box

ANSWERS ON PAGE 124

HINTS & TIPS

REMEMBER – IF YOU HAVEN'T GOT YOUR FOOT ON THE BRAKE WHEN YOU SELECT DRIVE IN AN AUTOMATIC CAR, THE VEHICLE MAY BEGIN TO MOVE FORWARD

SECTION 12

10 In which position should the gear selector be when you are starting the engine?

Answer _____ *or* _____

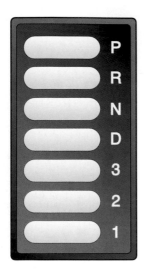

11 As you approach a bend, an automatic car will sometimes change up because there is less pressure on the accelerator.

What should you do to prevent this happening?

1 Slow down before the bend and accelerate gently as you turn. ☐

2 Brake as you go round the bend. ☐

3 Brake and accelerate at the same time. ☐

ANSWERS ON PAGE (124)

1 There are many myths and misunderstandings surrounding the driving test.

Are the following true or false? Tick the correct boxes   True False

1 The driving test is designed to see whether I can drive around a test route without making any mistakes.   ☐ ☐

2 The driving test is designed to see whether I can drive safely under various traffic conditions.   ☐ ☐

3 I do not need to know any of *The Highway Code.*   ☐ ☐

4 The examiner has a set allocation of passes each week.   ☐ ☐

5 I may be expected to drive up to the maximum national speed limit, where appropriate.   ☐ ☐

2 The length of the normal driving test is approximately ...

1 60 minutes   ☐

2 90 minutes   ☐

3 40 minutes   ☐

Tick the correct box

3 If, during the test, you do not understand what the examiner says to you, you would take a guess because you must not talk to him or her.

Is this statement true or false?   True False

Tick the correct box   ☐ ☐

ANSWERS ON PAGE 124

SECTION 13

4 You may have heard people say that it is easier to pass the driving test in certain parts of the country.

Do you agree with this statement?   Yes No

Tick the correct box   ☐ ☐

5 If you fail your test, you can take it again.

Which of the following statements is correct?

Tick the correct box(es)

1 If you fail the test, you can apply straight away for another appointment.   ☐

2 If you fail the test you have to wait a month before you can apply for another appointment.   ☐

3 You can re-take your test, subject to appointment availability, any time.   ☐

4 You have to wait 10 working days before you can re-take the test.   ☐

6 Before the practical part of your test, the examiner will test your eyesight.

This is done by asking you to read a number plate at a distance of ...

1 30.5 metres (100 feet)   ☐

2 20.5 metres (67 feet)   ☐

3 40.5 metres (133 feet)   ☐

Tick the correct box

ANSWERS ON PAGE (125)

SECTION 13

7 What will happen if you fail your eyesight test?

Answer _____

8 It is essential that you take both sections of your

p_ _ _ _ _ _ _ _ _ _ _ l_ _ _ _ _ _ to the test centre.

This document must be s_ _ _ _ _ in ink.

Complete the sentence

9 You will also be required to produce another form of identification; this

could be a p_ _ _ _ _ _ _ _ , or a photograph signed and

authorised by your i_ _ _ _ _ _ _ _ _.

10 The examiner will expect you to drive without making any mistakes.

Do you think this statement is true or false?

Tick the correct box

True False

☐ ☐

11 Is this statement about what you will be asked to do during the test true or false?

I will be asked to perform four set exercises:

1 The emergency stop

2 The turn in the road

3 Reversing into a side road on the right or left

4 Reverse parallel parking or reversing into a parking bay

Tick the correct box

True False

☐ ☐

☐ ☐

☐ ☐

☐ ☐

SECTION 13

ANSWERS ON PAGE 125

12 When reversing, are you allowed to undo your seat belt?

Tick the correct box

True   False
☐   ☐

13 If you fail your test, what will the examiner do?

1 _____

2 _____

14 When you have passed your driving test, what are you entitled to do?

1 _____

2 _____

3 _____

I5 I have within the last month passed my test.

Can I supervise a learner driver?

Tick the correct box

Yes   No
☐   ☐

16 When you pass your test, where should you send your pass certificate?

Answer _____

ANSWERS ON PAGE 125

SECTION 13

17 While you are waiting for your full licence to be sent to you, can you drive legally?

Yes   No

Tick the correct box

☐ ☐

18 It is recommended that you take further tuition once you have passed your test, especially on motorway driving.

As a learner driver you will not have experienced the special r_ _ _ _

that apply on the motorway and the h_ _ _ s_ _ _ _ of the other

traffic.

Complete the sentence

19 While taking your driving test, you should drive ...

1   Especially carefully, keeping about 5mph below the speed limit   ☐

2   As you would normally drive with your instructor   ☐

3   With confidence, keeping at or just over the speed limit, to show that you can really drive   ☐

Tick the correct box

20 Can you take a driving test if you are deaf?

Yes   No

Tick the correct box

☐ ☐

SECTION 13

ANSWERS ON PAGE 125

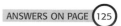

The driving test ensures that all drivers reach a minimum standard.

1 Do you think that learning to drive ends with passing the test?

Yes   No

Tick the correct box

☐ ☐

2 What knowledge and skills are not necessarily assessed in the present driving test?

List three

1 _____

2 _____

3 _____

3 Which of these statements do you think best describes advanced driving?

Tick the correct box

1 Advanced driving is learning to handle your car to its maximum performance. ☐

2 Advanced driving is learning to drive defensively with courtesy and consideration to others. ☐

3 Advanced driving is learning to drive fast. ☐

HINTS & TIPS

DRIVING IS A SKILL YOU CAN IMPROVE FOR THE REST OF YOUR LIFE; CONSIDER FURTHER TRAINING AFTER THE TEST.

ANSWERS ON PAGE 125

SECTION 14

4 Some people have difficulty in driving at night.

Which age group would you expect, in general, to experience most difficulties?

Tick the correct box

1   Older people ☐

2   Younger people ☐

5 Once you have passed your driving test, your licence is usually valid until you reach __ __ years of age.

Complete the sentence

6 There are particular circumstances under which you are required to take a driving test again.

Name them

Answer _____

_____

7 Motorways are designed to enable traffic to travel faster in greater safety.

Compared to other roads, are they statistically ...

1   Safer? ☐

2   Less safe? ☐

3   No different? ☐

Tick the correct box

SECTION 14

ANSWERS ON PAGE (125)

8 Are the following groups allowed on the motorway?

1 Provisional licence holders ☐

2 Motor cycles over 50cc ☐

3 Pedestrians ☐

4 HGV learner drivers ☐

5 Newly qualified drivers with less than three months' experience ☐

6 Motor cycles under 125cc ☐

7 Cyclists ☐

Tick the correct box

9 There are some routine checks you should carry out on your car before driving on the motorway.

Name four of them

1 _____   2 _____

3 _____   4 _____

10 On the motorway, if something falls from either your own or another vehicle, should you ...

1 Flash your headlights to inform other drivers? ☐

2 Pull over, put your hazard warning lights on and quickly run on to the motorway to collect the object? ☐

3 Pull over on to the hard shoulder, use the emergency telephone to call the police? ☐

4 Flag another motorist down to get help? ☐

Tick the correct box

ANSWERS ON PAGE 125

SECTION 14

11   Which colour do you associate with motorway signs?

1   Black lettering on a white background

2   White lettering on a green background

3   White lettering on a blue background

Tick the correct box

12   At night or in poor weather conditions, your headlights will pick out reflective studs. Match the colour of the studs to their function by placing the appropriate letter in the box.

A   AMBER   Marks the edge of the hard shoulder

B   RED   Marks the edge of the central reservation

C   GREEN   Marks the lane lines

D   WHITE   Marks exits and entrances

13   Do the broken lines at the end of the acceleration lane mean ...

1   The edge of the carriageway?

2   Other traffic should let you in?

3   Give way to traffic already on the carriageway?

Tick the correct box

SECTION 14

ANSWERS ON PAGE 126

14 If you see congestion ahead, is it legal to use your hazard warning lights to warn drivers behind you?

Tick the correct box

Yes No
☐ ☐

15 What is the most common cause of accidents on motorways?

1 Vehicles breaking down ☐

2 Drivers falling asleep ☐

3 Drivers travelling too fast, too close to the vehicle in front ☐

4 Fog ☐

Tick the correct box

16 Are the following statements true or false?

I can use the hard shoulder ...

True False

1 To take a short break ☐ ☐

2 To stop and read a map ☐ ☐

3 To allow the children to stretch their legs ☐ ☐

4 To pull over in an emergency ☐ ☐

5 To answer a phone call ☐ ☐

Tick the correct box

ANSWERS ON PAGE 126

SECTION 14

17 In normal driving on the motorway, you should overtake ...

1 On the right

2 On the left

3 On either side

Tick the correct box

Driving at night can cause problems.

18 Which of these statements do you think is correct?

Tick the correct box

1 Street lighting and my car's headlights mean that I can see just as well as in the daylight. Therefore driving at night is just like driving in the daylight.

2 At night I have to rely on my car's headlights and any additional lighting. Therefore I cannot see as far or drive as fast as in the daylight.

19 At dusk and dawn what action should you take to compensate for driving a dark coloured car?

Answer _____

20 When driving after dark in a built-up area, should you use ...

1 Dipped headlights?

2 Side or dim-dipped lights?

Tick the correct box

SECTION

14

ANSWERS ON PAGE 126

21 *The Highway Code* says you should not use your horn in a built-up area between 11.30pm and 7am.

What is the exception to that rule?

Answer _____

22 The diagram below illustrates two vehicles parked at night on a two-way road.

Which one is parked correctly?

 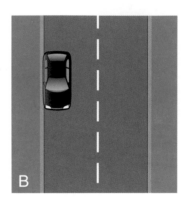

23 Certain groups of road users are particularly vulnerable at night.

Name two of them

1 _____   2 _____

24 Under what circumstances would you use dipped headlights during the day?

Answer _____

S__ __ and b__ s__ __ __.   *Complete the sentence*

ANSWERS ON PAGE (126)

SECTION 14

25 When you are waiting at a junction after dark, your brake lights might

d_ _ _ _ _ the driver behind. It is better to use your

h_ _ _ _ _ _ _ _.

Complete the sentences

Certain weather conditions can create hazardous driving conditions in the summer as well as in the winter.

26 Which of the following causes greatest danger to drivers?

Tick the correct box

1 Snow

2 Ice

3 Heavy rain

4 Not being able to see properly

27 In wet weather conditions your tyres can lose their grip.

You should allow at least d_ _ _ . _ _ _ the distance between you and

the car in front that you allow on a dry road.

Fill in the missing word

28 In very wet conditions there is a danger of a build-up of water between your tyres and the road.

This is called a_ _ _ _ _ _ _ _ _ _ _.

Fill in the missing word

SECTION 14

ANSWERS ON PAGE 126

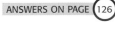

29 How can you prevent a build-up of water occurring?

S__ __ __ d__ __ __ .

30 How should you deal with floods?

Tick the correct box

1 Drive through as fast as possible to avoid stopping ☐

2 Drive through slowly in 1st gear, slipping the clutch to keep the engine speed high ☐

3 Drive through in the highest gear possible, slipping the clutch to keep the engine speed high ☐

31 Will less tread on your tyres ...

1 Increase your braking distance? ☐

2 Decrease your braking distance? ☐

Tick the correct box

32 When the tyres lose contact with the road, the steering will

feel v__ __ __ l__ __ __ __.

Complete the sentence

ANSWERS ON PAGE 126

33 After you have driven through a flood, should you check ...

1 Your speedometer? ☐

2 Your brakes? ☐

3 Your oil? ☐

Tick the correct box

34 There are certain key precautions you should take when driving in fog.

Complete the following sentences

1 S__ __ __ d__ __ __.

2 Ensure you are able to s__ __ __ within the distance you can see to be clear.

3 Use your w__ __ __ __ __ __ __ __ __ w__ __ __ __ __.

4 Use your d__ __ __ __ __ __ __ __ and your h__ __ __ __ __ r__ __ __ w__ __ __ __ __ __ __ __ __.

35 Under what circumstances should you use your rear fog lights?

When visibility is less than _____ metres/yards

Fill in the correct number

36 When you are following another vehicle in fog, should you ...

1 Follow closely behind because it will help you see where you are going? ☐

2 Leave plenty of room between you and the vehicle in front? ☐

Tick the correct box

ANSWERS ON PAGE 126

SECTION 14

37 When you are following another vehicle in fog, should you use ...

1   Main beam headlights?

2   Dipped headlights?

Tick the correct box

38 Extra precautions are needed when dealing with a junction in fog.

Complete the following sentences

1   Open your w__ __ __ __ __ __ and switch off your a__ __ __ __
s__ __ __ __ __. L__ __ __ __ __ for other vehicles.

2   Signal e__ __ __ __ .

3   Use your b__ __ __ __ __. The light will a__ __ __ __ following vehicles.

4   Use your h__ __ __ if you think it will w__ __ __ other road users.

39 Is the following statement about anti-lock brakes true or false?

Anti-lock brakes will stop me skidding when driving on snow or ice.

True False

Tick the correct box

40 When driving in snow or ice you should gently test your

b__ __ __ __ __ from time to time.

Fill in the missing word

ANSWERS ON PAGE 126

SECTION 14

41 In order to slow down when driving on snow or ice you should ...

  1 Use your brakes g__ __ __ __ __ .

  2 Get into a l__ __ __ __ __ g__ __ __ earlier than normal.

  3 Allow your speed to d__ __ __ and use b__ __ __ __ __ gently and early.

   Fill in the missing words

42 On snow or ice, braking distances can increase by ...

  1 10 times ☐

  2 5 times ☐

  3 20 times ☐

  4 15 times ☐

   Tick the correct box

43 When going downhill in snow, what would you do to help you slow down?

   Answer _____

44 When cornering in snow or ice, what should you avoid doing?

   Answer _____

45 How can you reduce the risk of wheel spin?

   Answer _____

SECTION 14

ANSWERS ON PAGE 126

46 Three important factors cause a skid

Name them

1 _____

2 _____

3 _____

HINTS & TIPS

IF YOU REALISE THAT YOUR CAR IS STARTING TO SKID, EASE OFF THE BRAKE AND ACCELERATOR, THEN STEER SMOOTHLY IN THE SAME DIRECTION AS THE SKID.

47 Some everyday driving actions, especially in poor weather, can increase the risk of skidding.

Fill in the missing words

1 S_ _ _ _ _ _ down.

2 S_ _ _ _ _ _ _ up.

3 T_ _ _ _ _ _ corners.

4 Driving u_ _ _ _ _ and d_ _ _ _ _ _ _ _.

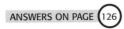 ANSWERS ON PAGE 126

All vehicles need routine attention and maintenance to keep them in good working order. Neglecting maintenance can be costly and dangerous.

1 With which of these statements do you agree?

Tick the correct box

1 Allowing the fuel gauge to drop too low is bad for the engine.

2 In modern cars the fuel level makes little difference.

2 What do you put into the engine to lubricate the moving parts?

Answer _____

3 How frequently should you check your oil level?

Tick the correct box

1 Once a month

2 Once a year

3 Every time you fill up with fuel

4 The engine is often cooled by a mixture of w_ _ _ _ _ and

a_ _ _ _ _ f_ _ _ _ _ _. Some engines are a_ _ cooled.

Complete the sentence

ANSWERS ON PAGE 127

5 How frequently should you test your brakes?

Tick the correct box

1 Daily ☐ 3 Weekly ☐

2 Monthly ☐ 4 When I use them ☐

6 Incorrectly adjusted headlamps can cause d_ _ _ _ _ to other road users.

Complete the sentence

7 All headlamps, indicators and brake lights should be kept in good working order.

It is also important that they are kept c_ _ _ _ .

Fill in the missing word

8 Tyres should be checked for u_ _ _ _ _ wear and tyre walls

for b_ _ _ _ _ and c_ _ _.

Complete the sentence

9 The legal requirement for tread depth is not less than ...

1 1.4mm ☐   2 1.6mm ☐   3 2mm ☐

Tick the correct box

ANSWERS ON PAGE (127)

10 What should you do if your brakes feel slack or spongy?

Answer _____

11 Vehicle breakdowns could result from ...

1 N__ __ __ __ __ __ of the vehicle
2 Lack of r__ __ __ __ __ __   c__ __ __ __ __
3 Little or no p__ __ __ __ __ __ __ __ __ __ __ maintenance
4 A__ __ __ __ of the vehicle

Fill in the missing words

12 **It is advisable to carry a warning triangle.**

1 On a straight road how far back should it be placed?

50 metres/yards ☐   200 metres/yards ☐   150 metres/yards ☐

Tick the correct box

2 On a dual carriageway, how far back should it be placed?
At least ...

200 metres/yards ☐   150 metres/yards ☐   450 metres/yards ☐

Tick the correct box

SECTION 15

ANSWERS ON PAGE 127

13 If you use a warning triangle, is it worth putting your hazard lights on as well?

Yes No

Tick the correct box ☐ ☐

14 If your vehicle breaks down on a motorway, should you ...

1 Gently brake, put your hazard lights on and seek assistance? ☐

2 Pull over to the central reservation as far to the right as possible? ☐

3 Pull over safely on to the hard shoulder as far away from the carriageway as possible? ☐

Tick the correct box

15 If your vehicle has broken down on the motorway, should you tell your passengers to ...

1 Stay in the vehicle while you seek assistance? ☐

2 Wait by the car on the hard shoulder but watch for other vehicles? ☐

3 Get out of the vehicle and wait on the embankment away from the hard shoulder? ☐

Tick the correct box

SECTION 15

ANSWERS ON PAGE (127)

16 The marker posts at the side of all motorways have a picture of a telephone handset.

How can you tell which way to walk to reach the nearest telephone?

Answer _____

_____

_____

17 When you use the emergency telephone on a motorway, what will the operator ask you?

1 _____

2 _____

3 _____

4 _____

18 Disabled drivers cannot easily get to an emergency telephone. How can they summon help?

1 _____

2 _____

SECTION 15

ANSWERS ON PAGE 127

19 If you break down when travelling alone, there are three things you are advised NOT to do.

Complete the sentences

1 Do not ask p__ __ __ __ __ __ m__ __ __ __ __ __ __ __ for help.

2 Do not accept help from anyone you d__ n__ __ k__ __ __ (except the emergency services or a breakdown service).

3 Do not l__ __ __ __ you vehicle l__ __ __ __ __ than necessary.

20 If I am first or one of the first to arrive at the scene of an accident, should I ...

	True	False
1 Always move injured people away from vehicles?	☐	☐
2 Tell the ambulance personnel or paramedics what I think is wrong with those injured?	☐	☐
3 Give casualties something warm to drink?	☐	☐
4 Switch off hazard warning lights?	☐	☐
5 Switch off vehicle engines?	☐	☐
6 Inform the police of the accident?	☐	☐

Tick the correct boxes

ANSWERS ON PAGE 127

21 If you are involved in an accident, what MUST you do?

Answer _____

22 If you are involved in an accident and nobody is injured, do you have to call the police?

Yes No
☐ ☐

Tick the correct box

SECTION 15

23 What information do you need to exchange if you are involved in an accident?

1 _____

2 _____

3 _____

4 _____

5 _____

24 If you thought you had a fire in your car's engine, what action would you take?

1 _____

2 _____

3 _____

25 There are three items of emergency equipment it is wise to carry in your car.

1 F_ _ _ _ A_ _ kit.

2 F_ _ _ e_ _ _ _ _ _ _ _ _ _ _.

3 W_ _ _ _ _ _ t_ _ _ _ _ _ _.

Fill in the missing words

SECTION

15

ANSWERS ON PAGE 127

26 When you rejoin a motorway from the hard shoulder, should you ...

1 Signal right and join when there is safe gap? ☐

2 Keep your hazard lights on and drive down the hard shoulder until there is a safe gap? ☐

3 Use the hard shoulder to build up speed and join the carriageway when safe? ☐

Tick the correct box

27 Fuel combustion causes waste products.

One of these is a gas called c__ __ __ __ __ d__ __ __ __ __ __. This is

a major cause of the g__ __ __ __ __ __ __ __ __ effect.

Complete the sentences

28 How much does transport contribute to the production of carbon dioxide in the country (expressed as a percentage of the total production)?

1 10 per cent ☐

2 25 per cent ☐

3 50 per cent ☐

4 20 per cent ☐

Tick the correct box

ANSWERS ON PAGE (127)

SECTION 15

29 The MOT test checks the roadworthiness of a vehicle.

Does it include an exhaust emission test?

Tick the correct box

Yes No
☐ ☐

30 A catalytic convertor stops the emission of carbon dioxide.

Tick the correct box

True False
☐ ☐

31 Which uses up more fuel?

1 A car travelling at 50mph ☐

2 A car travelling at 70mph ☐

Tick the correct box

32 There are some measures car drivers can take to help reduce damage to the environment.

List five

1 _____

2 _____

3 _____

4 _____

5 _____

SECTION 15

ANSWERS ON PAGE 127

Before buying a used car it is best to decide what you want the car for and how much you can afford.

33 There are three main sources of supply for used vehicles.

You can buy from a d_ _ _ _ _, at an a_ _ _ _ _ _ or

p_ _ _ _ _ _ _ _.

Complete the sentence

34 When reading a glowing description of a used car, what should you first consider?

Answer _____

35 Are these statements about buying a used car through a dealer or at an auction true or false?

		True	False
1	It is often cheaper to buy a car at an auction than through a dealer.	☐	☐
2	I have the same legal rights when I buy at an auction as when I buy from a dealer.	☐	☐
3	I should always read the terms and conditions of trade before I buy a car at an auction.	☐	☐
4	The best way to select a used car dealer is by recommendation.	☐	☐

Tick the correct boxes

ANSWERS ON PAGE 127

SECTION 15

36 Cars bought through a dealer often have a warranty.

What should you check?

1 _____

2 _____

37 When you test drive a vehicle, you should make sure that it is t_ _ _ _,

has a current M_ _ certificate (if applicable) and that

all i_ _ _ _ _ _ _ _ _ requirements are complied with.

Complete the sentence

38 There are some important items that you should check on before you buy a used car.

List three

1 _____

2 _____

3 _____

39 Do you think the following statement is true or false?

It is advisable to have my vehicle examined by a competent and unbiased expert before I buy.

True False
☐ ☐

Tick the correct box

ANSWERS ON PAGE 128

Particular difficulties are encountered when towing a caravan or trailer. There are some very good courses which will help master the skills required.

1 People can underestimate the length of the total combination of car and caravan or trailer.

Is the overall length usually ...

1 Twice the length of a normal car? ☐

2 Three times the length of a normal car? ☐

Tick the correct box

2 What additional fixtures should you attach to your car to help you see more clearly?

Answer _____

3 When towing you will need more distance than normal to overtake. Is it ...

1 Twice the normal distance? ☐

2 Three times the normal distance? ☐

3 Four times the normal distance? ☐

Tick the correct box

4 A device called a s__ __ __ __ __ __ __ __ __ __ will make the combination safer to handle.

Fill in the missing word

ANSWERS ON PAGE (128)

5 The stability of the caravan will depend on how you load it. Should heavy items be loaded ...

☐ **1** At the front?   ☐ **2** At the rear?   ☐ **3** Over the axle(s)?

Tick the correct box

6 There are special restrictions for vehicles which are towing.

A What is the speed limit on a dual carriageway?

Tick the correct box

☐ **1** 50mph   ☐ **2** 60mph   ☐ **3** 70mph

B What is the speed on a single carriageway?

Tick the correct box

☐ **1** 40mph   ☐ **2** 50mph   ☐ **3** 60mph

7 There are some important checks you should make before starting off.

List four

1 _____   2 _____

3 _____   4 _____

8 If you decide to stop to take a break, before allowing anyone to enter the caravan you should lower the j__ __ __ __ __ w__ __ __ __ and

c__ __ __ __ __ s__ __ __ __ __ __ __.

Fill in the missing words

ANSWERS ON PAGE (128)

Many people now take their car abroad or hire a vehicle when on holiday.

9 Motoring organisations, such as The Automobile Association, can help you plan and organise your trip.

The AA can provide advice on travel and v__ __ __ __ __ __ insurance.

They will also help you organise the d__ __ __ __ __ __ __ __ that you will need.

Fill in the missing words

10 Before travelling to Europe, you should always ...

1 Plan the r__ __ __ __ you wish to take.

2 Know the local m__ __ __ __ __ __ __ r__ __ __ __ __ __ __ __ __ __ __.

Complete the sentences

11 It is essential that your vehicle should be checked thoroughly.

List four of the routine checks you should make

1 _____

2 _____

3 _____

4 _____

ANSWERS ON PAGE 128

SECTION 16

12 In most European countries you are advised to carry your

d__ __ __ __ __ __   l__ __ __ __ __ __   on you.

Complete the sentence

13 What do the letters IDP stand for?

Answer _____

14 Where might you need an IDP?

Answer _____

15 In most European countries what age do you have to be to drive?

1 ☐   21   2 ☐   18   3 ☐   16

Tick the correct box

16 Some European countries can require you to carry additional emergency equipment.

List four of the items you are recommended to carry

1 _____

2 _____

3 _____

4 _____

ANSWERS ON PAGE 128

SECTION 16

Now you are the proud possessor of a full driving licence which allows you to drive vehicles up to 3.5 tonnes, use motorways for the first time, drive anywhere in the European Union and in many other countries worldwide, and to tow a small trailer. You are on your own dealing with whatever circumstances arise: fog, snow, ice, other drivers' mistakes. It is a huge responsibility.

Gaining experience is the key to a safe driving career. A new driver is at greater risk in the first two years following their test than at any other time. It is because of this that licence regulations stipulate that the accumulation of six or more penalty points during the first two years will mean the loss of a full driving licence and reversion to provisional status. This means that both theory and practical tests will have to be taken and passed all over again.

Having passed the driving test doesn't mean you have learnt everything there is to know; you will continue learning for the rest of your life. Consider some further training – this time without the comfort of L plates.

PASS PLUS

The Driving Standards Agency and the insurance industry recognise and seek to reward those new drivers who enhance their basic skills and widen their experience by taking further training in the form of the Pass Plus scheme.

This is a six-module syllabus which covers town and rural driving, night driving, driving in adverse conditions and motorway experience. An increasing number of insurance companies are prepared to offer discounts to new drivers who have completed the course.

Consider what real driving is all about; compare it to the type of driving you did when learning. There is little similarity. Your lesson is likely to have been about two hours long including stops for explanations, and you knew you could always fall back on the support of your instructor. Everyday driving involves driving in different areas, perhaps for extended periods, with only your own decisions to rely on.

Pass Plus provides a half-way solution. You have the benefit of your instructor's presence in a car you are familiar with, but this time in situations you are unfamiliar with, and with no L plates. It provides you with an opportunity to gain controlled experience.

MOTORWAY DRIVING

People learn to drive for a huge variety of reasons, but one reason that crops up time and time again is the freedom it allows. You will limit that freedom if you do not include the use of motorways as part of your experience. As a minimum but essential topic, you should have a lesson with your instructor on motorway driving, as this is the one road situation where up to now your training could not take place.

Contrary to popular belief, motorways are very safe roads when used properly. Only about 4% of accidents occur on motorways compared to 70% in urban areas. Learn how to use them safely.

You will have already realised that the faster you drive, the faster you must think and be able to react. Motorways are faster roads, so you must develop greater observation, anticipation and planning skills. Because you are effectively driving on a one-way road often for long distances and durations, levels of concentration must also be maintained.

The maximum speed on a motorway is 70mph; this is a maximum not a target. Even though some drivers ignore this limit, you must not be pulled along by other traffic into dangerous and illegal situations. Drive at a speed with which you are comfortable, but recognise that it would also be dangerous to hinder the progress of others.

Joining and leaving motorways are often the situations that less experienced drivers find most daunting. You already know the theory and the rules, but they have to be put into practice. The first time you do this on your own, make sure it is on a quiet stretch of motorway. Leave at the very next exit and rejoin immediately; this will build up your experience much more quickly.

SECTION

17

Boredom and fatigue can also affect safe driving on motorways. Do not drive for a long time without taking a break. In the early stages 'a long time' may be a mere half-hour, but even when you become more experienced, the time between breaks should not be more than two hours.

It is estimated that a high percentage of motorway accidents can be attributed to fatigue, and worse still, to falling asleep. Excluding those with sleep disorders, people know when they are tired or fighting sleep. This is not the time to carry on driving. Take a break, take a nap.

YOU – THE CAR – THE ENVIRONMENT

Owning and running a car is an expensive business. The cost is not just measured in the price of the fuel you buy, but in the wider consequences of cost to the environment. Every driver can take some simple actions which will help everyone.

On a daily basis ask yourself: do you really need to make that short car journey? Once a week check that tyres are correctly inflated; not only will wrong pressures wear the tyres more quickly, but under-inflation will increase fuel consumption.

Look after the vehicle you drive, make sure it is serviced regularly and the engine correctly tuned. Not only will this help to keep pollution to a minimum but also to make sure fuel is burnt efficiently. Remove excess weight from your vehicle; even an empty roof rack will increase fuel consumption by about 5%.

The way you drive also affects the volume of fuel that the engine burns. By driving smoothly and avoiding sudden acceleration or braking, fuel is not wasted and you and your passengers have a more comfortable ride. By driving at 70mph up to 30% more fuel would be used than driving at 50mph. Use speed appropriately and economically.

Sue Hubbard
Business Development Manager, AA The Driving School

Section 1

INTRODUCTION TO LEARNING TO DRIVE
Questions on pages 12–13

A1
A current, signed, full or provisional licence for the category of vehicle that you are driving

A2
examinations
register

A3
21 years old
three years

A4
To the front and rear. It is important not to place them in windows where they could restrict good vision.

A5
True

A6
You should have answered No to all the questions.

A7
Yes. This should be the ambition of every driver.

A8   3, 4

ADJUSTING YOUR DRIVING POSITION
Questions on page 14

A9
1 handbrake
2 doors
3 seat
4 head restraint
5 mirrors
6 seat belt

INTRODUCTION TO VEHICLE CONTROLS
Questions on pages 14–15

A10
The handbrake	E
The driving mirrors	D
The gear lever	F
The clutch	G
The steering wheel	A
The foot-brake	B
The accelerator	C

A11
The foot-brake	R
The clutch	L
The accelerator	R

A12
1 False. You will need one hand to change gear or use other controls.
2 True
3 False. The best position is quarter to three or ten to two.
4 False. It is safest to feed the wheel through your hands.
5 True
6 True

A13
The direction indicators	B
Dipped beam	A
Main beam	D
Rear fog lamp	C
Horn	E
Hazard lights	F

Section 2

MOVING OFF
Questions on page 16

A1
A	1
B	5
C	3
D	2

E	6
F	4
G	7
H	8
I	9

STOPPING (NORMALLY)
Questions on page 17

A2
A	1
B	3
C	2
D	4
E	6
F	5
G	8
H	7
I	9

GEAR CHANGING
Questions on pages 18–20

A3
1st gear

A4
5th, or 4th if the car has a 4-speed gear box

A5
Usually 2nd gear, but 1st if you need to go very slowly or 3rd if the corner is sweeping and you can take it safely at a higher speed

A6
engine
vehicle
sound
when

A7
A	1
B	3
C	2
D	4
E	5

A8
1 False. This will cause the engine to labour.
2 False. It is good practice to use the brakes to slow the car down. Using the transmission causes wear and tear which can be very costly. Also, the brakes are more effective.
3 False
4 True
5 False. It is good practice to miss out the unwanted gears and select the gear most appropriate to your road speed.

A9   1

A10
1 Don't
2 Don't
3 Do
4 Do
5 Do
6 Don't
7 Don't
8 Don't

STEERING
Questions on page 21

A11
A, except in a few cars fitted with four-wheel steering (in which case all four wheels will move)

A12 A

A13 B

A14 B

ROAD POSITIONING
Questions on page 22

A15
C well to the left but not too close to the kerb

A16
B. Avoid swerving in and out. It is unnecessary and confuses other drivers.

CLUTCH CONTROL
Questions on page 23

A17 A

A18 biting

A19
1 Yes
2 Yes
3 No
4 Yes
5 No

Section 3

JUNCTIONS
Questions on pages 24–7

A1
two or more roads

A2
A T-junction
B Y-junction
C Roundabout
D Staggered crossroads
E Crossroads

A3
1 E
2 C
3 B
4 D
5 A

A4
A 1
B 3

A5
1 Mirrors
2 Signal
3 Position
4 Speed
5 Look

A6
assess
decide
act

A7 A

A8 B

A9 D

A10
1 mirrors, position
2 signal
3 safe
4 safe distance
5 overtake

CROSSROADS
Questions on page 28

A11
A 3 Crossroads. Priority for traffic on the major road. Never assume other drivers will give you priority.
B 1 Unmarked crossroads
C 2 Crossroads with give way lines at the end of your road. Give way to traffic on the major road.

ROUNDABOUTS
Questions on pages 29–31

A12 C

A13
1 Left
2 Left
3 Right. Remember to use the MSM routine before signalling left to turn off.

A14
1 Left

2 Going ahead
3 Right

A15
mirrors
signal
position
speed
look

A16 2

Section 4

PARKING (ON THE ROAD)
Questions on pages 32–3

A1
1 safe
2 considerate
3 legal

A2
Cars 1, 2, 3, 6

A3
1 False
2 False
3 True
4 True

A4
Any of the following:
at a bus stop
at a school entrance
opposite a junction
on a bend
on the brow of a hill
on a Clearway
on a motorway
at night facing oncoming traffic
in a residents' parking zone.

Section 5

PASSING STATIONARY VEHICLES AND OBSTRUCTIONS
Questions on page 34

A1
Vehicle 2

A2
Vehicle 2, even though the obstruction is on the right. Where safe, when travelling downhill be prepared to give priority to vehicles (especially heavy vehicles) that are coming uphill.

MEETING AND CROSSING THE PATH OF OTHER VEHICLES
Questions on pages 35–6

A3
1 True
2 False. Always consider whether it is safe. Are there dangers the other driver cannot see? Remember, flashing headlamps has the same meaning as sounding the horn. It is a warning: 'I am here!' Sometimes it is taken to mean: 'I am here and I am letting you pass.'
3 True

A4
1 Yes
2 Yes
3 No
4 Yes
5 Yes
6 Yes
7 Yes

Section 6

STOPPING IN AN EMERGENCY
Questions on pages 37–8

A1
1 True
2 True
3 True
4 False. Looking in the mirror should not be necessary. You should know what is behind you.
5 False
6 True
7 True

A2
False. An emergency stop will be conducted randomly on only some tests. You must always know how to stop safely in an emergency.

A3
pump
1 maximum
2 lock
3 quickly

A4
steer
brake
pump
pressure

1 False. Other elements beyond braking can cause skidding e.g. acceleration or going too fast into a bend.
2 False. Although you may stop in a shorter distance, you still need to leave the correct distance to allow yourself time to react and vehicles behind you time to stop.

STOPPING DISTANCES
Questions on pages 39–40

A5
1 No
2 Yes
3 Yes
4 No

ANSWERS

18

A6 ½ second

A7
1 23 metres/75 feet
2 15 metres/50 feet
3 96 metres/315 feet

A8
longer
more

A9
breaks
two-second

Section 7

MOVING OFF AT AN ANGLE
Question on page 41

A1
1 False. You should check your mirrors and blindspot before moving out. Keep alert for other traffic as you pull out and stop if necessary.
2 True
3 False. Move out slowly and carefully.
4 True. The closer you are, the greater the angle.
5 True. As you move out, you are likely to move on to the right-hand side of the road and into conflict with oncoming vehicles.
6 False. You should signal only if it helps or warns other road users. Signalling gives you no right to pull out.

MOVING OFF UPHILL
Question on page 42

A2
1 True
2 False. Using the accelerator pedal will not move the car forwards.

3 False. As your feet will be using the clutch pedal and the accelerator pedal you need to use the handbrake to stop the car rolling back.
4 True
5 True
6 True
7 True

MOVING OFF DOWNHILL
Question on page 43

A3
1 True
2 False. Almost certainly you will need to use the foot-brake.
3 False. It is often better to move off in 2nd gear.
4 True. This will stop the car rolling forwards.
5 True
6 False. You will need to have your foot on the foot-brake to stop the car rolling forwards.

APPROACHING JUNCTIONS UPHILL AND DOWNHILL
Question on page 44

A4
The following statements are correct:
1, 4, 5, 6, 7

Section 8

REVERSING
Questions on pages 45–7

A1
safe
convenient
law

A2
1 False
2 False

3 True
4 True

A3   A

A4   1, 4

A5
Car A: to the left
Car B: to the right

A6
observation

REVERSING INTO A SIDE ROAD ON THE LEFT
Questions on pages 47–8

A7   3

A8
1 True
2 False
3 True

A9   4

A10   C

A11   Left

A12
The front of the car will swing out to the right

A13
1 True
2 False
3 True

A14
pedestrians
road users
stop

REVERSING INTO A SIDE ROAD ON THE RIGHT
Questions on pages 49–50

A15   True

A16 B

A17 2

A18
True. You may need to place your left hand at 12 o'clock and lower your right hand.

A19 True

A20 2

A21 B

TURNING IN THE ROAD
Questions on pages 51–3

A22 A

A23
slowly
briskly

A24
False, but you should try to complete the manoeuvre in as few moves as possible.

A25 2, 3, 4

A26
all round

A27
1 Right
2 Steer briskly left
3 Left
4 Steer briskly right
5 Right

A28
1 Left
2 Over your right shoulder to where the car is going

REVERSE PARALLEL PARKING
Questions on pages 54–7

A29 2

A30
C, in line with the rear of the parked vehicle

A31 2

A32
1 To the left
2 The nearside headlamp of the vehicle towards which you are reversing
3 Clipping the rear offside of the lead car
4 Take off the left lock
5 Steer to the right and then take off the right lock as you get straight

A33
1 False
2 False
3 True. You will be expected to be able to complete the exercise within approximately two car lengths.

A34
All round, particularly for pedestrians and oncoming vehicles

A35
C. The other bay widths are reduced by parked vehicles. This may make opening doors a squeeze.

A36
Allows you to make best use of the area in front of the bay
Gives you a better view when driving out of the space

A37
close
directions
pedestrians

Section 9

TRAFFIC LIGHTS AND YELLOW BOX JUNCTIONS
Questions on pages 58–60

A1
1 red
2 red and amber
3 green
4 amber
5 red

A2
1 green
2 red and amber
3 amber
4 red

A3
1 False
2 True
3 True
4 False.
Pedestrians who are already crossing have priority.

A4 2

A5
1 Lane A or B
2 Lane C
3 Lane A

A6
1 No   ⎤ If your exit is blocked
        ⎥ you should not enter a
2 No   ⎦ yellow box junction.

3 Yes

ANSWERS 18

PEDESTRIAN CROSSINGS
Questions on pages 60–3

A7
1 Zig-zag lines
2 Flashing yellow beacons on both sides of the road
3 Black and white stripes on the crossing
4 A give way line

A8
1 True
2 True. You must not park or wait on the zig-zag lines on either side of the crossing.
3 False. You must not overtake on the zig-zag lines on approach to the crossing.
4 True
5 True. A slowing down arm signal should be used. It helps pedestrians understand what you intend to do. They cannot see your brake lights.

A9
1 Traffic lights
2 Zig-zag lines
3 A white stop line

A10
2 A white stick means the pedestrian is visually handicapped. A white stick with two reflector bands means the pedestrian may be deaf as well as visually handicapped.

A11
1 Flashing amber
2 You must give way to pedestrians on the crossing, but if it is clear you may go on.

A12
A bleeping tone. This sounds when the red light shows to drivers and helps visually handicapped pedestrians know when it is safe to cross.

A13
There is no flashing amber light sequence. The light sequence is the same as normal traffic lights.

A14 cyclists

LEVEL CROSSINGS
Questions on page 63

A15

A   3
B   1
C   2
D   4

A16
2
4
5

Section 10

ONE-WAY SYSTEMS
Questions on page 64

A1
A is the correct sign for a one-way street.
B tells you 'Ahead only'.

A2
1 True
2 True
3 True
4 True

ROAD MARKINGS
Questions on pages 64–7

A3
information
warnings
orders

A4
1 They can be seen when other signs may be hidden
2 They give a continuing message

A5

A 2
B 2

A6
1, 4

A7
They are used to separate potentially dangerous streams of traffic.

A8
You must not enter the hatched area.

TRAFFIC SIGNS
Questions on pages 67–8

A9
1 Warning
2 Order
3 Information

A10
1 must
2 must not

A11
1 You must give way to traffic on the major road. Delay your entry until it is safe to join the major road.
2 You must stop (even if the road is clear). Wait until you can enter the new road safely.

A12
vision is limited

A13
Motorway signs   D
Primary routes   E

Other routes   B
Local places   C
Tourist signs   A

Section 11

ROAD OBSERVATION
Questions on pages 69–71

A1
speed
behaviour
intentions

A2
1 Observe that the view into the new road is restricted.
The driver should ...
Move forward slowly, to get a better view.
Note the pedestrian who may walk in front of or behind car A.
Note the pedestrian waiting to cross.
   Allow the cyclist to pass.
Once in position to see car B, stop and give way.
2 Observe that the parked car restricts the view into and out of the side road.
The driver should ...
Slow down on approach to parked car P.
Take up position to gain a better view and be more visible to car A and the pedestrian.
Slow down in case the pedestrian walks out from behind the parked car P.
Consider signal to pass parked car P.
Look carefully into minor road.
   Note the actions of car A. Be prepared to stop.

A3   bike

A4
3, but touching the brakes may encourage the driver to drop back

A5
A
1 Junctions
2 Hump-back bridges
3 Concealed entrances
4 Dead ground
5 Narrow lanes

B
1 Children playing
2 Horses
3 Pedestrians
4 Especially elderly and young cyclists
5 Other vehicles

A6
1 True. The ability to advise those at your destination of delays can help to reduce the worry of late arrivals
2 True
3 True
4 True

A7
All are distracting and upset concentration, and should not be carried out while driving.

DEALING WITH BENDS
Questions on pages 71–2

A8
speed
gear
position

A9   1

A10   B

A11   A

A12
A On a right-hand bend keep to the left. This will help to improve your view.
B On a left-hand bend keep to the centre of the lane. Do not move to the centre of the road to get a better view. A vehicle travelling in the opposite direction may be taking the bend wide.

OVERTAKING
Questions on pages 73–4

A13
necessary
1 Mirrors
2 Position
3 Speed
4 Look
5 Mirrors
6 Signal
7 Manoeuvre

A14
About the width of a small car, more in windy or poor weather conditions

A15
1 The vehicle in front is signalling and positioned to turn right
2 You are using the correct lane to turn left at a junction
3 Traffic is moving slowly in queues and the traffic on the right is moving more slowly than you are
4 You are in a one-way street

A16
1 On approach to a junction
2 The brow of a hill
3 The approach to a bend
4 Where there is dead ground.
   NB These are examples. Be guided by *The Highway Code*.

DUAL CARRIAGEWAYS
Questions on pages 74–6

A17
2. Statements 1, 3, 4 and 5 do not apply:
1 Reflective studs are used on some dual carriageways.
3 The speed limit is subject to local conditions and may vary from 40mph up to the national speed limit.
4 You can turn right on to and off dual carriageways unlike motorways, where all traffic enters and leaves on the left.
5 You may find slow moving vehicles sometimes displaying a flashing amber light.

A18
A You would cross over the first carriageway then wait in the gap in the central reservation. Be careful, if you are towing or if your vehicle is long, that you do not cause other road users to change course or slow down.
B You would wait until there is a gap in the traffic long enough for you safely to clear the first carriageway and emerge into the second.

A19
The speed limit applies to all lanes. Use the first lane to travel in and the second for overtaking.

A20
A Dual carriageway ends
B Road narrows on both sides
C Two-way traffic straight ahead

A21
A and C

A22
Traffic is moving much faster, and one or more lanes will have to be crossed.

Section 12

DRIVING AN AUTOMATIC CAR
Questions on pages 77–80

A1
Clutch

A2
1 Driving is easier
2 There is more time to concentrate on the road

A3
Park – Locks the transmission. This should be selected only when the vehicle is stationary.
Reverse – Enables the car to go backwards, as in a manual car.
Neutral – Has the same function as in a manual car. The engine is not in contact with the driving wheels.
Drive – Is used for driving forwards. It automatically selects the most appropriate gear.
3rd, 2nd, 1st } Have the same function as manual gears

A4 3

A5
1 Yes
2 No
3 Yes, if you needed extra control
4 You would probably use kickdown, but possibly in certain circumstances you would manually select a lower gear
5 Yes, maybe using 1st gear
6 No. Use the brakes

A6
1 The right foot
2 The right foot

A7
It stops you trying to control the brake and accelerator at the same time. It encourages early release of the accelerator and progressive braking.

A8
Drive, reverse, all forward gears.

A9
1 You should apply the handbrake every time you stop. Otherwise you have to keep your foot on the foot-brake.

A10
Park (P) or Neutral (N)

A11 1

Section 13

THE DRIVING TEST
Questions on pages 81–5

A1
1 False
2 True
3 False
4 False
5 True

A2 3

A3
False. If you did not hear clearly or did not understand what the examiner said, you should ask him or her to repeat the instruction. If you have any problem with your hearing, it is advisable to tell the examiner at the start of the test.

A4

No. The standard test does not vary. The test result should be the same wherever it is taken.

A5 1, 4

A6 2

A7

The test will not proceed. You have failed not only the eyesight section, but the whole test. Remember, if you wear glasses or contact lenses, to wear them for the eyesight test and for the rest of the driving test.

A8

provisional licence
signed

A9

passport
instructor

A10

False. You can make some minor errors and still reach the required standard.

A11

False. Only about one third of test candidates will be asked to complete an emergency stop. You will be asked to do two out of the three reversing manoeuvres.

A12

Yes, but remember to do it up again when you have completed the exercise.

A13

1 Give you a verbal explanation of the main reasons for failure
2 Write out a form for you to take away showing you your main errors

A14

1 Drive unsupervised
2 Drive on a motorway
3 Drive without L-plates

A15

No. You must have had at least three years' driving experience (and be over 21 years of age).

A16

To the DVLA, Swansea

A17

Yes. It is a good idea to keep a note of your driver number and the date you passed your test.

A18

rules
high speed

A19

2 The examiner will expect you to drive normally. You should abide by all speed limits and drive according to road and traffic conditions.

A20

Yes. The examiner will be skilled in giving instructions and directions to deaf candidates.

Section 14

BEYOND THE TEST
Questions on pages 86–7

A1

No

A2

1 Bad weather driving
2 Night-time driving
3 Motorway driving
4 Skid control ... and more

A3 2

A4

1, although people of any age can find it difficult to drive at night

A5 70

A6

There are certain serious driving offences which carry the penalty of disqualification. In order to regain a full licence, the disqualified driver has to apply for a provisional licence and take an extended test. If, because of certain illnesses, you have been unable to drive for 10 years, you will be required to take the test again in order to gain a full licence.

For new drivers: the accumulation of six or more penalty points within two years of passing the test will mean reverting to a provisional licence and re-sitting the test.

MOTORWAY DRIVING
Questions on pages 87–91

A7 1

A8

1 No
2 Yes
3 No
4 Yes
5 Yes
6 Yes
7 No

A9

1 Oil
2 Water
3 Fuel
4 Tyre pressures
    These are just some of the checks; for more information, refer to your car's manual.

ANSWERS 18

ANSWERS

A10
3 You should never attempt to retrieve anything from the carriageway.

A11 3

A12
B Amber
A Red
D Green
C White

A13 3

A14 Yes

A15 3

A16
1 False
2 False
3 False
4 True
5 False

A17
1, except when traffic is moving slowly in queues and the queue on the right is travelling more slowly

SAFE NIGHT DRIVING
Questions on pages 91–3

A18 2

A19
Switch on earlier, switch off later.

A20
1. It helps others to see you.

A21
If you are stationary, to avoid danger from a moving vehicle.

A22
A. Always park with the flow of traffic. You will show red reflectors to vehicles travelling in your direction.

A23
1 Pedestrians
2 Cyclists
3 Motor cyclists
} two of these

A24
In poor weather conditions – see and be seen

A25
dazzle
handbrake

ALL-WEATHER DRIVING
Questions on pages 93–98

A26 4

A27
double

A28
aquaplaning

A29
Slow down
Allow time for the tread patterns to disperse the water.

A30 2

A31 1

A3   very light

A33 2

A34
1 Slow down
2 stop
3 windscreen wipers
4 demister, heated rear windscreen

A35
100 metres/yards

A36 2

A37 2

A38
1 windows, audio system. Listen
2 early
3 brakes, alert
4 horn, warn

A39
False, because your tyres are not in contact with the road

A40
brakes

A41
1 gently
2 lower gear
3 drop, brakes

A42 1

A43
If possible, control your speed before reaching the hill. Select a low gear early.

A44
Using your brakes

A45
Avoid harsh acceleration

A46
1 The driver
2 The vehicle
3 The road conditions

A47
1 Slowing
2 Speeding
3 Turning
4 uphill, downhill

Section 15

VEHICLE CARE
Questions on pages 99–100

A1 1

A2 Oil

A3 3

A4
Water, anti-freeze, air

A5 1

A6
dazzle

A7
clean

A8
uneven, bulges, cuts

A9 2

A10
Get them checked as quickly as possible.

BREAKDOWNS, ACCIDENTS AND EMERGENCIES
Questions on pages 101–6

A11
1 Neglect
2 routine checks
3 preventative
4 abuse

A12
1 50 metres/yards
2 At least 150 metres/yards

A13
Yes. Try to give as much warning as possible.

A14 3

A15 3

A16
Under the drawing of the handset is an arrow which points to the nearest telephone.

A17
1 The emergency number (painted on the box)
2 Vehicle details (make, registration mark, colour)
3 Membership details of your motoring organisation
4 Details of the fault

A18
1 By displaying a Help pennant
2 By using a mobile telephone

A19
1 passing motorists
2 do not know
3 leave, longer

A20
1 False. Do not move injured people unless they are in danger.
2 False. Tell them the facts, not what you think is wrong.
3 False. Do not give those injured anything to eat or drink. Keep them warm and reassure them.
4 False. Keep hazard lights on to warn other drivers.
5 True. Switch off engines. Put out cigarettes.
6 True, in the case of injury.

A21
Stop

A22 No

A23
1 The other driver's name, address and contact number

2 The registration numbers of all vehicles involved
3 The make of the other car
4 The other driver's insurance details
5 If the driver is not the owner, the owner's details.

A24
1 Pull up quickly
2 Get all passengers out
3 Call assistance

A25
1 First aid
2 Fire extinguisher
3 Warning triangle

A26 3

THE MOTOR CAR AND THE ENVIRONMENT
Questions on pages 106–7

A27
carbon dioxide, greenhouse

A28 4

A29 Yes

A30
False. A catalytic convertor reduces the level of carbon monoxide, nitrogen oxide and hydrocarbons by up to 90 per cent. Carbon dioxide is still produced.

A31 2

A32
Nine measures are listed here:
1 Make sure your vehicle is in good condition and regularly serviced.
2 Make sure tyres are correctly inflated. Under-inflated tyres waste fuel.

ANSWERS 18

3 Push the choke in as soon as possible when starting from cold.

4 Avoid harsh braking.

5 Buy a fuel-efficient vehicle.

6 Use the most appropriate gear.

7 Use your accelerator sensibly and avoid harsh acceleration.

8 Use unleaded fuel.

9 Dispose of waste oil, old batteries and used tyres sensibly.

BUYING A USED CAR
Questions on pages 108–9

A33

dealer, auction, privately

A34

Why is it being sold?

A35

1 True

2 False

3 True

4 True

A36

1 What is covered

2 The length of the agreement

A37

taxed, MOT, insurance

A38

Four items to check are listed here:

1 Mileage

2 Has it been involved in any accidents?

3 Number of owners

4 Is there any hire purchase or finance agreement outstanding?

A39

True. The AA offer a national inspection scheme.

Section 16

TOWING A CARAVAN OR TRAILER
Questions on pages 110–11

A1 1

A2

Exterior towing mirrors, to give you a good view

A3 2

A4

stabilizer

A5 3

A6

A   2

B   2

A7

Seven checks are listed here:

1 Is the caravan or trailer loaded correctly?

2 Is it correctly hitched up to your vehicle?

3 Are the lights and indicators working properly?

4 Is the braking system working correctly?

5 Is the jockey wheel assembly fully retracted?

6 Are tyre pressures correct?

7 Are all windows, doors and roof lights closed?

A8

jockey wheel, corner steadies

DRIVING IN EUROPE
Questions on pages 112–3

A9

vehicle, documents

A10

1 route

2 motoring regulations

A11

Here are five routine checks:

1 Tyres, including spare. Always carry a spare tyre.

2 Tool kit and jack.

3 Lamps and brake lights.

4 Fit deflectors to your headlamps to prevent dazzle to other drivers approaching on the left.

5 Check you have an extra exterior mirror on the left.

A12

driving licence

A13

International Driving Permit

A14

Some non-EU countries

A15 2

A16

Five items are listed here:

1 Spare lamps and bulbs

2 Warning triangle

3 First aid kit

4 Fire extinguisher

5 Emergency windscreen

Contents PAGE

Introduction

The Highway Code is essential reading for everyone. Its rules apply to all road users: pedestrians, horse riders and cyclists, as well as motorcyclists and drivers.

Many of the rules in the Code are legal requirements, and if you disobey these rules you are committing a criminal offence. You may be fined, given penalty points on your licence or be disqualified from driving. In the most serious cases you may be sent to prison. Such rules are identified by the use of the words **MUST/MUST NOT**. In addition, the rule includes an abbreviated reference to the legislation which creates the offence. An explanation of the abbreviations is in Annexe 4: The road user and the law.

Although failure to comply with the other rules of the Code will not, in itself, cause a person to be prosecuted, *The Highway Code* may be used in evidence in any court proceedings under the Traffic Acts to establish liability.

Knowing and applying the rules contained in *The Highway Code* could significantly reduce road accident casualties. Cutting the number of deaths and injuries that occur on our roads every day is a responsibility we all share. *The Highway Code* can help us discharge that responsibility.

Rules for pedestrians

General guidance

1. Pavements or footpaths should be used if provided. Where possible, avoid walking next to the kerb with your back to the traffic. If you have to step into the road, look both ways first.

2. If there is no pavement or footpath, walk on the right-hand side of the road so that you can see oncoming traffic. You should take extra care and

- be prepared to walk in single file, especially on narrow roads or in poor light
- keep close to the side of the road.

It may be safer to cross the road well before a sharp right-hand bend (so that oncoming traffic has a better chance of seeing you). Cross back after the bend.

3. Help other road users to see you. Wear or carry something light coloured, bright or fluorescent in poor daylight conditions. When it is dark, use reflective materials (e.g. armbands, sashes, waistcoats and jackets), which can be seen, by drivers using headlights, up to three times as far away as non-reflective materials.

Be seen in the dark; wear something reflective

4. Young children should not be out alone on the pavement or road (see Rule 7). When taking children out, walk between them and the traffic and hold their hands firmly. Strap very young children into push-chairs or use reins.

5. Organised walks. Groups of people should use a path if available; if one is not, they should keep to the left. Look-outs should be positioned at the front and back of the group, and they should wear fluorescent clothes in daylight and reflective clothes in the dark. At night, the look-out in front should carry a white light and the one at the back a red light. People on the outside of large groups should also carry lights and wear reflective clothing.

6. Motorways. You **MUST NOT** walk on motorways or slip roads except in an emergency (see Rule 249).

Laws RTRA sect 17, MT(E&W)R 1982 as amended & MT(S)R regs 2 & 13

Crossing the road

7. The Green Cross Code. The advice given below on crossing the road is for all pedestrians. Children should be taught the Code and should not be allowed out alone until they can understand and use it properly. The age when they can do this is different for each child. Many children cannot judge how fast vehicles are going or how far away they are. Children learn by example, so parents and carers should always use the Code in full when out with their children. They are responsible for deciding at what age children can use it safely by themselves.

a. First find a safe place to cross. It is safer to cross using a subway, a footbridge, an island, a zebra, pelican, toucan or puffin crossing, or where there is a crossing point controlled by a police officer, a school crossing patrol or a traffic warden. Where there is a crossing nearby, use it. Otherwise choose a place where you can see clearly in all directions. Try to avoid crossing between parked cars (see Rule 14) and on blind bends and brows of hills. Move to a space where drivers can see you clearly.

b. Stop just before you get to the kerb, where you can see if anything is coming. Do not get too close to the traffic. If there is no pavement, keep back from the edge of the road but make sure you can still see approaching traffic.

c. Look all around for traffic and listen. Traffic could come from any direction. Listen as well, because you can sometimes hear traffic before you see it.

d. If traffic is coming, let it pass. Look all around again and listen. Do not cross until there is a safe gap in the traffic and you are certain that there is plenty of time. Remember, even if traffic is a long way off, it may be approaching very quickly.

e. When it is safe, go straight across the road – do not run. Keep looking and listening for traffic while you cross, in case there is any traffic you did not see, or in case other traffic appears suddenly.

8. At a junction. When crossing the road, look out for traffic turning into the road, especially from behind you.

9. Pedestrian Safety Barriers. Where there are barriers, cross the road only at the gaps provided for pedestrians. Do not climb over the barriers or walk between them and the road.

10. Tactile paving. Small raised studs which can be felt underfoot may be used to advise blind or partially-sighted people that they are approaching a crossing point with a dropped kerb.

11. One-way streets. Check which way the traffic is moving. Do not cross until it is safe to do so without stopping. Bus and cycle lanes may operate in the opposite direction to the rest of the traffic.

12. Bus and cycle lanes. Take care when crossing these lanes as traffic may be moving faster than in the other lanes, or against the flow of traffic.

13. Routes shared with cyclists. Cycle tracks may run alongside footpaths, with a dividing line segregating the two. Keep to the section for pedestrians. Take extra care where cyclists and pedestrians share the same path without separation (see Rule 48).

14. Parked vehicles. If you have to cross between parked vehicles, use the outside edges of the vehicles as if they were the kerb. Stop there and make sure you can see all around and that the traffic can see you. Never cross the road in front of, or behind, any vehicle with its engine running, especially a large vehicle, as the driver may not be able to see you.

15. Reversing vehicles. Never cross behind a vehicle which is reversing, showing white reversing lights or sounding a warning.

16. Moving vehicles. You **MUST NOT** get on to or hold on to a moving vehicle.
Law RTA 1988 sect 26

17. At night. Wear something reflective to make it easier for others to see you (see Rule 3). If there is no pedestrian crossing nearby, cross the road near a street light so that traffic can see you more easily.

Crossings

18. At all crossings. When using any type of crossing you should
- always check that the traffic has stopped before you start to cross or push a pram on to a crossing
- always cross between the studs or over the zebra markings. Do not cross at the side of the crossing or on the zig-zag lines, as it can be dangerous.

You **MUST NOT** loiter on zebra, pelican or puffin crossings.
Laws ZPPPCRGD reg 19 & RTRA sect 25(5)

19. Zebra crossings. Give traffic plenty of time to see you and to stop before you start to cross. Vehicles will need more time when the road is slippery. Remember that traffic does not have to stop until someone has moved on to the crossing. Wait until traffic has stopped from both directions or the road is clear before crossing. Keep looking both ways, and listening, in case a driver or rider has not seen you and attempts to overtake a vehicle that has stopped.

20. Where there is an island in the middle of a zebra crossing, wait on the island and follow Rule 19 before you cross the second half of the road – it is a separate crossing.

21. At traffic lights. There may be special signals for pedestrians. You should only start to cross the road when the green figure shows. If you have started to cross the road and the green figure goes out, you should still have time to reach the other side, but do not delay. If no pedestrian signals have been provided, watch carefully and do not cross until the traffic lights are red and the traffic has stopped. Keep looking and check for traffic that may be turning the corner. Remember that traffic lights may let traffic move in some lanes while traffic in other lanes has stopped.

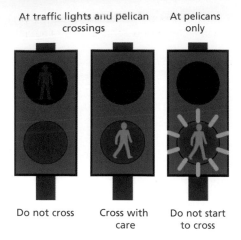

At traffic lights and pelican crossings

At pelicans only

Do not cross

Cross with care

Do not start to cross

Pedestrian signals at traffic lights and pelican crossings

22. Pelican crossings. These are signal-controlled crossings operated by pedestrians. Push the control button to activate the traffic signals. When the red figure shows, do not cross. When a steady green figure shows, check the traffic has stopped then cross with care. When the green figure begins to flash you should not start to cross. If you have already started you should have time to finish crossing safely.

23. At some pelican crossings there is a bleeping sound to indicate to blind or partially-sighted people when the steady green figure is showing, and there may be a tactile signal to help deafblind people.

24. When the road is congested, traffic on your side of the road may be forced to stop even though their lights are green. Traffic may still be moving on the other side of the road, so press the button and wait for the signal to cross.

25. Puffin and toucan crossings. These differ from pelican crossings as there is no flashing green figure phase. On puffin crossings the red and green figures are above the control box on your side of the road. Press the button and wait for the green figure to show. On toucan crossings cyclists are permitted to ride across the road (see Rule 65).

26. 'Staggered' pelican or puffin crossings. When the crossings on each side of the central refuge are not in line they are two separate crossings. On reaching the central island press the button again and wait for a steady green figure.

27. Crossings controlled by an authorised person. Do not cross the road unless you are signalled to do so by a police officer, traffic warden or school crossing patrol. Always cross in front of them.

28. Where there are no controlled crossing points available it is advisable to cross where there is an island in the middle of the road. Use the Green Cross Code to cross to the island and then stop and use it again to cross the second half of the road.

Situations needing extra care

29. Emergency vehicles. If an ambulance, fire engine, police or other emergency vehicle approaches using flashing blue lights, headlights and/or sirens, keep off the road.

30. Buses. Get on or off a bus only when it has stopped to allow you to do so. Watch out for cyclists when you are getting off. Never cross the road directly behind or in front of a bus; wait until it has moved off and you can see clearly in both directions.

31. Tramways. These may run through pedestrian areas. Their path will be marked out by shallow kerbs, changes in the paving or other road surface, white lines or yellow dots. Cross at designated crossings where provided. Flashing amber lights may warn you that a tram is approaching. Elsewhere look both ways along the track before crossing. Do not walk along the track. Trams move quickly and silently and cannot steer to avoid you.

32. Railway level crossings. Do not cross if the red lights show, an alarm is sounding or the barriers are being lowered. The tone of the alarm will change if another train is approaching. If there are no lights, alarms or barriers, stop, look both ways and listen before crossing.

33. Street and pavement repairs. A pavement may be closed temporarily because it is not safe to use. Take extra care if you are directed to walk in or to cross the road.

Rules about animals

Horseriders

34. Safety equipment. Children under the age of 14 **MUST** wear a helmet which complies with the Regulations. It **MUST** be fastened securely. Other riders should also follow this advice.
Law H(PHYR)R

35. Other clothing. You should wear
- boots or shoes with hard soles and heels
- light-coloured or fluorescent clothing in daylight
- reflective clothing if you have to ride at night or in poor visibility.

36. At night. It is safer not to ride on the road at night or in poor visibility, but if you do, make sure your horse has reflective bands above the fetlock joints. Carry a light which shows white to the front and red to the rear.

Riding

37. Before you take a horse on to a road, you should
- ensure all tack fits well and is in good condition
- make sure you can control the horse.

Always ride with other, less nervous horses if you think that your horse will be nervous of traffic. Never ride a horse without a saddle or bridle.

38. Before riding off or turning, look behind you to make sure it is safe, then give a clear arm signal.

39. When riding on the road you should
- keep to the left
- keep both hands on the reins unless you are signalling
- keep both feet in the stirrups
- not carry another person
- not carry anything which might affect your balance or get tangled up with the reins
- keep a horse you are leading to your left
- move in the direction of the traffic flow in a one-way street
- never ride more than two abreast, and ride in single file where the road narrows or on the approach to a bend.

40. You **MUST NOT** take a horse on to a footpath, pavement or cycle track. Use a bridleway where possible.
Laws HA 1835 sect 72 & R(S)A sect 129(5)

41. Avoid roundabouts wherever possible. If you use them you should
- keep to the left and watch out for vehicles crossing your path to leave or join the roundabout
- signal right when riding across exits to show you are not leaving
- signal left just before you leave the roundabout.

Other animals

42. Dogs. Do not let a dog out on the road on its own. Keep it on a short lead when walking on the pavement, road or path shared with cyclists.

43. When in a vehicle make sure dogs or other animals are suitably restrained so they cannot distract you while you are driving or injure you if you stop quickly.

44. Animals being herded. These should be kept under control at all times. You should, if possible, send another person along the road in front to warn other road users, especially at a bend or the brow of a hill. It is safer not to move animals after dark, but if you do, then wear reflective clothing and ensure that lights are carried (white at the front and red at the rear of the herd).

Rules for cyclists

These rules are in addition to those in the following sections, which apply to all vehicles (except the motorway section). See also Annexe 1: Choosing and maintaining your bicycle.

45. Clothing. You should wear
- a cycle helmet which conforms to current regulations
- appropriate clothes for cycling. Avoid clothes which may get tangled in the chain, or in a wheel or may obscure your lights
- light-coloured or fluorescent clothing which helps other road users to see you in daylight and poor light
- reflective clothing and/or accessories (belt, arm or ankle bands) in the dark.

Help yourself to be seen

46. At night your cycle **MUST** have front and rear lights lit. It **MUST** also be fitted with a red rear reflector (and amber pedal reflectors, if manufactured after 1/10/85). White front reflectors and spoke reflectors will also help you to be seen.
Law RVLR regs 18 & 24

When cycling
47. Use cycle routes when practicable. They can make your journey safer.

48. Cycle Tracks. These are normally located away from the road, but may occasionally be found alongside footpaths or pavements. Cyclists and pedestrians may be segregated or they may share the same space (unsegregated). When using segregated tracks you **MUST** keep to the

side intended for cyclists. Take care when passing pedestrians, especially children, elderly or disabled people, and allow them plenty of room. Always be prepared to slow down and stop if necessary.
Law HA 1835 sect 72

49. Cycle Lanes. These are marked by a white line (which may be broken) along the carriageway (see Rule 119). Keep within the lane wherever possible.

50. You **MUST** obey all traffic signs and traffic light signals.
Laws RTA 1988 sect 36, TSRGD reg 10(1)

51. You should
- keep both hands on the handlebars except when signalling or changing gear
- keep both feet on the pedals
- not ride more than two abreast
- ride in single file on narrow or busy roads
- not ride close behind another vehicle
- not carry anything which will affect your balance or may get tangled up with your wheels or chain
- be considerate of other road users, particularly blind and partially-sighted pedestrians. Let them know you are there when necessary, for example by ringing your bell.

52. You should
- look all around before moving away from the kerb, turning or manoeuvring, to make sure it is safe to do so. Give a clear signal to show other road users what you intend to do (see Signals to other road users)
- look well ahead for obstructions in the road, such as drains, pot-holes and parked vehicles so that you do not have to swerve suddenly to avoid them. Leave plenty of room when passing parked vehicles and watch out for doors being opened into your path
- take extra care near road humps, narrowings and other traffic calming features.

53. You **MUST NOT**
- carry a passenger unless your cycle has been built or adapted to carry one
- hold on to a moving vehicle or trailer
- ride in a dangerous, careless or inconsiderate manner
- ride when under the influence of drink or drugs.
Law RTA 1988 sects 24, 26, 28, 29 & 30 as amended by RTA 1991

54. You **MUST NOT** cycle on a pavement. Do not leave your cycle where it would endanger or obstruct road users or pedestrians, for example, lying on the pavement. Use cycle parking facilities where provided.
Laws HA 1835 sect 72 & R(S)A sect 129

55. You **MUST NOT** cross the stop line when the traffic lights are red. Some junctions have an advanced stop line to enable you to position yourself ahead of other traffic (see Rule 154).
Laws RTA 1988 sect 36, TSRGD regs 10 & 36(1)

56. Bus Lanes. These may be used by cyclists only if the signs include a cycle symbol. Watch out for people getting on or off a bus. Be very careful when overtaking a bus or leaving a bus lane as you will be entering a busier traffic flow.

Road junctions

57. On the left. When approaching a junction on the left, watch out for vehicles turning in front of you, out of or into the side road. Do not ride on the inside of vehicles signalling or slowing down to turn left.

58. Pay particular attention to long vehicles which need a lot of room to manoeuvre at corners. They may have to move over to the right before turning left. Wait until they have completed the manoeuvre because the rear wheels come very close to the kerb while turning. Do not be tempted to ride in the space between them and the kerb.

59. On the right. If you are turning right, check the traffic to ensure it is safe, then signal and move to the centre of the road. Wait until there is a safe gap in the oncoming traffic before completing the turn. It may be safer to wait on the left until there is a safe gap or to dismount and push your cycle across the road.

60. Dual carriageways. Remember that traffic on most dual carriageways moves quickly. When crossing wait for a safe gap and cross each carriageway in turn. Take extra care when crossing slip roads.

Roundabouts

61. Full details about the correct procedure at roundabouts are contained in Rules 160–166. Roundabouts can be hazardous and should be approached with care.

62. You may feel safer either keeping to the left on the roundabout or dismounting and walking your cycle round on the pavement or verge. If you decide to keep to the left you should

- be aware that drivers may not easily see you
- take extra care when cycling across exits and you may need to signal right to show you are not leaving the roundabout
- watch out for vehicles crossing your path to leave or join the roundabout.

63. Give plenty of room to long vehicles on the roundabout as they need more space to manoeuvre. Do not ride in the space they need to get round the roundabout. It may be safer to wait until they have cleared the roundabout.

Crossing the road
64. Do not ride across a pelican, puffin or zebra crossing. Dismount and wheel your cycle across.

65. Toucan crossings. These are light-controlled crossings which allow cyclists and pedestrians to cross at the same time. They are push button operated. Pedestrians and cyclists will see the green signal together. Cyclists are permitted to ride across.

66. Cycle-only crossings. Cycle tracks on opposite sides of the road may be linked by signalled crossings. You may ride across but you **MUST NOT** cross until the green cycle symbol is showing.
Law TSRGD reg 36(1)

Rules for motorcyclists

These Rules are in addition to those in the following sections which apply to all vehicles. For motorcycle licence requirements see Annexe 2: Motorcycle licence requirements.

General

67. On all journeys, the rider and pillion passenger on a motorcycle, scooter or moped **MUST** wear a protective helmet. Helmets **MUST** comply with the Regulations and they **MUST** be fastened securely. It is also advisable to wear eye protectors, which **MUST** comply with the Regulations. Consider wearing ear protection. Strong boots, gloves and suitable clothing may help to protect you if you fall off.

Laws RTA 1988 sects 16 &17 & MC(PH)R as amended reg 4, & RTA sect 18 & MC(EP)R as amended reg 4

68. You **MUST NOT** carry more than one pillion passenger and he/she **MUST** sit astride the machine on a proper seat and should keep both feet on the footrests.

Law RTA 1988 sect 23

69. Daylight riding. Make yourself as visible as possible from the side as well as the front and rear. You could wear a white or brightly-coloured helmet. Wear fluorescent clothing or strips. Dipped headlights, even in good daylight, may also make you more conspicuous.

Make sure you can be seen

70. Riding in the dark. Wear reflective clothing or strips to improve your chances of being seen in the dark. These reflect light from the headlamps of other vehicles making you more visible from a long distance. See Rules 93–96 for lighting requirements.

71. Manoeuvring. You should be aware of what is behind and to the sides before manoeuvring. Look behind you; use mirrors if they are fitted. When overtaking traffic queues look out for pedestrians crossing between vehicles and vehicles emerging from junctions.
Remember: Observation – Signal – Manoeuvre.

Rules for drivers and motorcyclists

72. Vehicle condition. You **MUST** ensure your vehicle and trailer complies with the full requirements of the Road Vehicles (Construction and Use) Regulations and Road Vehicles Lighting Regulations. (See Annexe 6: Vehicle maintenance safety and security).

73. Before setting off. You should ensure that
- you have planned your route and allowed sufficient time
- clothing and footwear do not prevent you using the controls in the correct manner
- you know where all the controls are and how to use them before you need them. All vehicles are different; do not wait until it is too late to find out
- your mirrors and seat are adjusted correctly to ensure comfort, full control and maximum vision
- head restraints are properly adjusted to reduce the risk of neck injuries in the event of an accident
- you have sufficient fuel before commencing your journey, especially if it includes motorway driving. It can be dangerous to lose power when driving in traffic.

74. Vehicle towing and loading. As a driver
- you **MUST NOT** tow more than your licence permits you to
- you **MUST NOT** overload your vehicle or trailer. You should not

tow a weight greater than that recommended by the manufacturer of your vehicle

- you **MUST** secure your load and it **MUST NOT** stick out dangerously
- you should properly distribute the weight in your caravan or trailer with heavy items mainly over the axle(s) and ensure a downward load on the tow ball. Manufacturer's recommended weight and tow ball load should not be exceeded. This should avoid the possibility of swerving or snaking and going out of control. If this does happen, ease off the accelerator and reduce speed gently to regain control.

Law CUR reg 100, MV(DL)R reg 43

Seat Belts

75. You **MUST** wear a seat belt if one is available, unless you are exempt. Those exempt from the requirement include the holders of medical exemption certificates and people making local deliveries in a vehicle designed for the purpose.

Laws RTA 1988 sects 14 & 15, MV(WSB)R & MV(WSBCFS)R

Seat belt requirements

This table summarises the main legal requirements for wearing seat belts

	FRONT SEAT (all vehicles)	REAR SEAT (cars and small minibuses*)	WHOSE RESPONSIBILITY
DRIVER	**MUST** be worn if fitted		DRIVER
CHILD under 3 years of age	Appropriate child restraint **MUST** be worn	Appropriate child restraint **MUST** be worn *if available*	DRIVER
CHILD aged 3 to 11 and under 1.5 metres (about 5 feet) in height	Appropriate child restraint **MUST** be worn *if available.* If not, an adult seat belt **MUST** be worn	Appropriate child restraint **MUST** be worn *if available.* If not, an adult seat belt **MUST** be worn *if available*	DRIVER
CHILD aged 12 or 13 or younger child 1.5 metres or more in height	Adult seat belt **MUST** be worn *if available*	Adult seat belt **MUST** be worn *if available*	DRIVER
PASSENGER over the age of 14	**MUST** be worn *if available*	**MUST** be worn *if available*	PASSENGER

*Minibuses with an unladen weight of 2540kg or less

76. The driver **MUST** ensure that all children under 14 years of age wear seat belts or sit in an approved child restraint. This should be a baby seat, child seat, booster seat or booster cushion appropriate to the child's weight and size, fitted to the manufacturer's instructions.
Laws RTA 1988 sects 14 & 15, MV(WSB)R & MV(WSBCFS)R

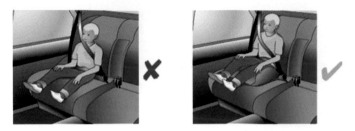

Make sure children wear the correct restraint

77. You **MUST** wear seat belts in minibuses with an unladen weight of 2540 kg or less. You should wear them in large minibuses and coaches where available.
Laws RTA 1988 sects 14 & 15, MV(WSB)R & MV(WSBCFS)R

78. Children in cars. Drivers who are carrying children in cars should ensure that
- children do not sit behind the rear seats in an estate car or hatchback, unless a special child seat has been fitted
- the child safety door locks, where fitted, are used when children are in the car
- children are kept under control
- a rear-facing baby seat is **NEVER** fitted into a seat protected by an airbag.

Fitness to drive
79. Make sure that you are fit to drive. You **MUST** report to the Driver and Vehicle Licensing Agency (DVLA) any health condition likely to affect your driving.
Law RTA 1988 sect 94

80. Driving when you are tired greatly increases your accident risk. To minimise this risk
- make sure you are fit to drive. Do not undertake a long journey (longer than an hour) if you feel tired
- avoid undertaking long journeys between midnight and 6am, when natural alertness is at a minimum

- plan your journey to take sufficient breaks. A minimum break of at least 15 minutes after every two hours of driving is recommended
- if you feel at all sleepy, stop in a safe place. Do not stop on the hard shoulder of a motorway
- the most effective ways to counter sleepiness are to take a short nap (up to 15 minutes) or drink, for example, two cups of strong coffee. Fresh air, exercise or turning up the radio may help for a short time, but are **not** as effective.

81. Vision. You **MUST** be able to read a vehicle number plate from a distance of 20.5 metres (67 feet – about five car lengths) in good daylight. From September 2001, you **MUST** be able to read a new style number plate from a distance of 20 metres (66 feet). If you need to wear glasses (or contact lenses) to do this, you **MUST** wear them at all times whilst driving. The police have the power to require a driver, at any time, to undertake an eyesight test in good daylight.
Laws RTA 1988 sect 96 & MV(DL)R reg 40 & sch 8

82. At night or in poor visibility, do not use tinted glasses, lenses or visors or anything that restricts vision.

Alcohol and drugs
83. Do not drink and drive as it will seriously affect your judgement and abilities. You **MUST NOT** drive with a breath alcohol level higher than 35 µg /100 ml or a blood alcohol level of more than 80 mg/100 ml. Alcohol will
- give a false sense of confidence
- reduce co-ordination and slow down reactions
- affect judgement of speed, distance and risk
- reduce your driving ability, even if you are below the legal limit
- take time to leave your body; you may be unfit to drive in the evening after drinking at lunchtime, or in the morning after drinking the previous evening. If you are going to drink, arrange another means of transport.
Law RTA 1988 sects 4, 5 & 11(2)

84. You **MUST NOT** drive under the influence of drugs or medicine. Check the instructions or ask your doctor or pharmacist. Using illegal drugs is highly dangerous. Never take them before driving; the effects are unpredictable, but can be even more severe than alcohol and may result in fatal or serious road accidents.
Law RTA 1988 sect 4

General rules, techniques and advice for all drivers and riders

This section should be read by all drivers, motorcyclists and cyclists. The rules in *The Highway Code* do not give you the right of way in any circumstance, but they advise you when you should give way to others. Always give way if it can help to avoid an accident.

Signals

85. Signals warn and inform other road users, including pedestrians (see Signals to other road users), of your intended actions.

You should
- give clear signals in plenty of time, having checked it is not misleading to signal at that time
- use them, if necessary, before changing course or direction, stopping or moving off
- cancel them after use
- make sure your signals will not confuse others. If, for instance, you want to stop after a side road, do not signal until you are passing the road. If you signal earlier it may give the impression that you intend to turn into the road. Your brake lights will warn traffic behind you that you are slowing down
- use an arm signal to emphasise or reinforce your signal if necessary. Remember that signalling does not give you priority.

86. You should also
- watch out for signals given by other road users and proceed only when you are satisfied that it is safe
- be aware that an indicator on another vehicle may not have been cancelled.

87. You **MUST** obey signals given by police officers and traffic wardens (see Signals by authorised persons) and signs used by school crossing patrols.
Laws RTRA sect 28, RTA 1988 sect 35 and FTWO art 3

Traffic light signals and traffic signs
88. You **MUST** obey all traffic light signals (see Light signals controlling traffic) and traffic signs giving orders, including temporary signals and signs (see Traffic Signs and Road works signs). Make sure you know, understand and act on all other traffic and information signs and road

markings (see Traffic signs and Road markings).

Laws RTA 1988 sect 36, TSRGD regs 10,15,16,25,26,27,28,29,36,38 & 40

89. Police stopping procedures. If the police want to stop your vehicle they will, where possible, attract your attention by
- flashing blue lights or headlights or sounding their siren or horn
- directing you to pull over to the side by pointing and/or using the left indicator.

You **MUST** then pull over and stop as soon as it is safe to do so. Then switch off your engine.

Law RTA 1988 sect 163

90. Flashing headlights. Only flash your headlights to let other road users know that you are there. Do not flash your headlights in an attempt to intimidate other road users.

91. If another driver flashes his headlights never assume that it is a signal to go. Use your own judgement and proceed carefully.

92. The horn. Use only while your vehicle is moving and you need to warn other road users of your presence. Never sound your horn aggressively. You **MUST NOT** use your horn
- while stationary on the road
- when driving in a built-up area between the hours of 11.30 pm and 7.00 am

except when another vehicle poses a danger.

Law CUR reg 99

Lighting requirements

93. You **MUST**
- use headlights at night, except on restricted roads (those with street lights not more than 185 metres (600 feet) apart and which are generally subject to a speed limit of 30 mph)
- use headlights when visibility is seriously reduced (see Rule 201)
- ensure all sidelights and rear registration plate lights are lit at night.

Laws RVLR regs 24 & 25 & RV(R&L)R reg 19

94. You **MUST NOT**
- use any lights in a way which would dazzle or cause discomfort to other road users
- use front or rear fog lights unless visibility is seriously reduced. You **MUST** switch them off when visibility improves to avoid dazzling other road users.

Law RVLR reg 27

95. You should also

- use dipped headlights, or dim-dip if fitted, at night in built-up areas and in dull daytime weather, to ensure that you can be seen
- keep your headlights dipped when overtaking until you are level with the other vehicle and then change to main beam if necessary, unless this would dazzle oncoming traffic
- slow down, and if necessary stop, if you are dazzled by oncoming headlights.

96. Hazard warning lights. These may be used when your vehicle is stationary, to warn that it is temporarily obstructing traffic. Never use them as an excuse for dangerous or illegal parking. You **MUST NOT** use hazard warning lights whilst driving unless you are on a motorway or unrestricted dual carriageway and you need to warn drivers behind you of a hazard or obstruction ahead. Only use them for long enough to ensure that your warning has been observed.

Law RVLR reg 27

Control of the vehicle
Braking

97. In normal circumstances. The safest way to brake is to do so early and lightly. Brake more firmly as you begin to stop. Ease the pressure off just before the vehicle comes to rest to avoid a jerky stop.

98. In an emergency. Brake immediately. Try to avoid braking so harshly that you lock your wheels. Locked wheels can lead to skidding.

99. Skids. Skidding is caused by the driver braking, accelerating or steering too harshly or driving too fast for the road conditions. If skidding occurs, ease off the brake or accelerator and try to steer smoothly in the direction of the skid. For example, if the rear of the vehicle skids to the right, steer quickly and smoothly to the right to recover.

Rear of car skids to the right

Driver steers to the right

100. ABS. The presence of an anti-lock braking system should not cause you to alter the way you brake from that indicated in Rule 97. However in the case of an emergency, apply the footbrake rapidly and firmly; do not release the pressure until the vehicle has slowed to the desired speed. The ABS should ensure that steering control will be retained.

101. Brakes affected by water. If you have driven through deep water your brakes may be less effective. Test them at the first safe opportunity by pushing gently on the brake pedal to make sure that they work. If they are not fully effective, gently apply light pressure while driving slowly. This will help to dry them out.

102. Coasting. This term describes a vehicle travelling in neutral or with the clutch pressed down. Do not coast, whatever the driving conditions. It reduces driver control because
- engine braking is eliminated
- vehicle speed downhill will increase quickly
- increased use of the footbrake can reduce its effectiveness
- steering response will be affected particularly on bends and corners
- it may be more difficult to select the appropriate gear when needed.

Speed limits
103. You **MUST NOT** exceed the maximum speed limits for the road and for your vehicle (see the table on the next page). Street lights usually mean that there is a 30 mph speed limit unless there are signs showing another limit.

Law RTRA sects 81,86,89 & sch 6

Speed Limits

Type of vehicle	Built-up areas*	Elsewhere		Motorways
		Single carriageways	Dual carriageways	
	MPH	MPH	MPH	MPH
Cars & motorcycles (including car derived vans up to 2 tonnes maximum laden weight)	30	60	70	70
Cars towing caravans or trailers (including car derived vans and motorcycles)	30	50	60	60
Buses & coaches (not exceeding 12 metres in overall length)	30	50	60	70
Goods vehicles (not exceeding 7.5 tonnes maximum laden wieght)	30	50	60	70†
Goods vehicles (exceeding 7.5 tonnes maximum laden wieght)	30	40	50	60

These are the national speed limits and apply to all roads unless signs show otherwise.
*The 30mph limit applies to all traffic on all roads in England and Wales (only class C and unclassified roads in Scotland) with street lighting unless signs show otherwise.
†60 if articulated or towing a trailer

104. The speed limit is the absolute maximum and does not mean it is safe to drive at that speed irrespective of conditions. Driving at speeds too fast for the road and traffic conditions can be dangerous. You should always reduce your speed when

- the road layout or condition presents hazards, such as bends
- sharing the road with pedestrians and cyclists, particularly children, and motorcyclists
- weather conditions make it safer to do so
- driving at night as it is harder to see other road users.

Stopping distances

105. Drive at a speed that will allow you to stop well within the distance you can see to be clear. You should

- leave enough space between you and the vehicle in front so that you can pull up safely if it suddenly slows down or stops. The safe rule is never to get closer than the overall stopping distance (see Typical Stopping Distances diagram, on the next page)
- allow at least a two-second gap between you and the vehicle in front on roads carrying fast traffic. The gap should be at least doubled on wet roads and increased still further on icy roads
- remember, large vehicles and motorcycles need a greater distance to stop.

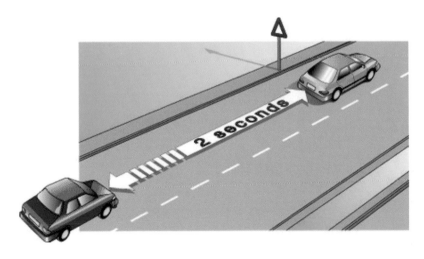

Use a fixed point to help measure a two-second gap

Typical stopping Distances

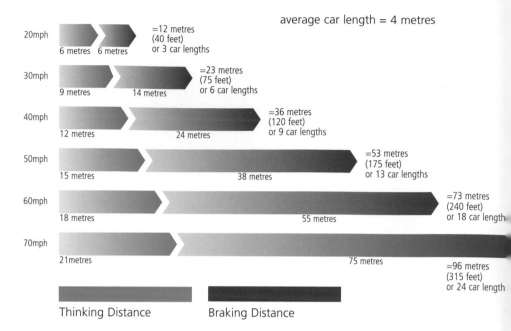

average car length = 4 metres

20mph — 6 metres, 6 metres = 12 metres (40 feet) or 3 car lengths

30mph — 9 metres, 14 metres = 23 metres (75 feet) or 6 car lengths

40mph — 12 metres, 24 metres = 36 metres (120 feet) or 9 car lengths

50mph — 15 metres, 38 metres = 53 metres (175 feet) or 13 car lengths

60mph — 18 metres, 55 metres = 73 metres (240 feet) or 18 car length

70mph — 21 metres, 75 metres = 96 metres (315 feet) or 24 car length

Thinking Distance   Braking Distance

Lines and lane markings on the road

Diagrams of all lines shown in Road markings.

106. A broken white line. This marks the centre of the road. When this line lengthens and the gaps shorten, it means that there is a hazard ahead. Do not cross it unless you can see the road is clear well ahead and wish to overtake or turn off.

107. Double white lines where the line nearest to you is broken. This means you may cross the lines to overtake if it is safe, provided you can complete the manoeuvre before reaching a solid white line on your side. White arrows on the road indicate when you need to get back onto your side of the road.

108. Double white lines where the line nearest you is solid. This means you **MUST NOT** cross or straddle it unless it is safe and you need to enter adjoining premises or a side road. You may cross the line if necessary to pass a stationary vehicle, or overtake a pedal cycle, horse or road maintenance vehicle, if they are travelling at 10 mph or less.

Laws RTA sect 36 & TSRGD regs 10 & 26

109. Areas of white diagonal stripes or chevrons painted on the road. These are to separate traffic lanes or to protect traffic turning right.

- If the area is bordered by a broken white line, you should not enter the area unless it is necessary and you can see that it is safe to do so.
- If the area is marked with diagonal stripes and bordered by solid white lines, you should not enter it except in an emergency.
- If the area is marked with chevrons and bordered by solid white lines you **MUST NOT** enter it except in an emergency.

Laws MT(E&W)R regs 5,9,10 & 16, MT(S)R regs 4,8,9 & 14, RTA sect 36 & TSRGD 10(1)

110. Lane dividers. These are short broken white lines which are used on wide carriageways to divide them into lanes. You should keep between them.

111. Reflective road studs may be used with white lines.

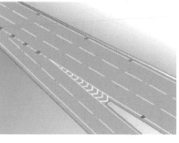

- White studs mark the lanes or the middle of the road.
- Red studs mark the left edge of the road.
- Amber studs mark the central reservation of a dual carriageway or motorway.
- Green studs mark the edge of the main carriageway at lay-bys, side roads and slip roads.

Multi-lane carriageways
Lane discipline

112. If you need to change lane, first use your mirrors and check your blind spots (the areas you are unable to see in the mirrors) to make sure you will not force another driver or rider to swerve or slow down. When it is safe to do so, signal to indicate your intentions to other road users and when clear move over.

113. You should follow the signs and road markings and get into lane as directed. In congested road conditions do not change lanes unnecessarily.

Single carriageway

114. Where a single carriageway has three lanes and the road markings or signs do not give priority to traffic in either direction
- use the middle lane only for overtaking or turning right. Remember, you have no more right to use the middle lane than a driver coming from the opposite direction
- do not use the right-hand lane.

115. Where a single carriageway has four or more lanes, use only the lanes that signs or markings indicate.

Dual carriageways

116. On a two-lane dual carriageway you should stay in the left-hand lane. Use the right-hand lane for overtaking or turning right. If you use it for overtaking move back to the left-hand lane when it is safe to do so.

117. On a three-lane dual carriageway, you may use the middle lane or the right-hand lane to overtake but return to the middle and then the left-hand lane when it is safe.

118. Climbing and crawler lanes. These are provided on some hills. Use this lane if you are driving a slow moving vehicle or if there are vehicles behind you wishing to overtake.

119. Cycle lanes. These are shown by road markings and signs. You **MUST NOT** drive or park in a cycle lane marked by a solid white line during its times of operation. Do not drive or park in a cycle lane marked by a broken white line unless it is unavoidable. You **MUST NOT** park in any cycle lane whilst waiting restrictions apply.

Law RTRA sects 5 & 8

120. Bus and tram lanes. These are shown by road markings and signs. You **MUST NOT** drive or stop in a tram lane or in a bus lane during its period of operation unless the signs indicate you may do so.
Law RTRA sects 5 & 8

121. One-way streets. Traffic **MUST** travel in the direction indicated by signs. Buses and/or cycles may have a contraflow lane. Choose the correct lane for your exit as soon as you can. Do not change lanes suddenly. Unless road signs or markings indicate otherwise, you should use
- the left-hand lane when going left
- the right-hand lane when going right
- the most appropriate lane when going straight ahead.

Remember – traffic could be passing on both sides.
Laws RTA 1988 sect 36 & RTRA sects 5 & 8

General advice

122. You MUST NOT
- drive dangerously
- drive without due care and attention
- drive without reasonable consideration for other road users.

Law RTA 1988 sects 2 & 3 as amended by RTA 1991

123. You **MUST NOT** drive on or over a pavement, footpath or bridleway except to gain lawful access to property.
Laws HA 1835 sect 72 & RTA sect 34

124. Adapt your driving to the appropriate type and condition of road you are on. In particular
- do not treat speed limits as a target. It is often not appropriate or safe to drive at the maximum speed limit
- take the road and traffic conditions into account. Be prepared for unexpected or difficult situations, for example, the road being blocked beyond a blind bend. Be prepared to adjust your speed as a precaution
- where there are junctions, be prepared for vehicles emerging
- in side roads and country lanes look out for unmarked junctions where nobody has priority
- try to anticipate what pedestrians and cyclists might do.
  If pedestrians, particularly children, are looking the other way, they may step out into the road without seeing you.

125. Be considerate. Be careful of and considerate towards other road users. You should
- try to be understanding if other drivers cause problems; they may be inexperienced or not know the area well
- be patient; remember that anyone can make a mistake
- not allow yourself to become agitated or involved if someone is behaving badly on the road. This will only make the situation worse. Pull over, calm down and, when you feel relaxed, continue your journey
- slow down and hold back if a vehicle pulls out into your path at a junction. Allow it to get clear. Do not over-react by driving too close behind it.

126. Safe driving needs concentration. Avoid distractions when driving such as
- loud music (this may mask other sounds)
- trying to read maps
- inserting a cassette or CD or tuning a radio
- arguing with your passengers or other road users
- eating and drinking.

Mobile phones and in-car technology
127. You **MUST** exercise proper control of your vehicle at all times. You **MUST NOT** use a hand-held mobile phone, or similiar device, when driving or when supervising a learner driver, except to call 999 or 112 in a genuine emergency when it is unsafe or impractical to stop. Never use a hand-held microphone when driving. Using hands-free equipment is also likely to distract your attention from the road. It is far safer not to use any telephone while you are driving – find a safe place to stop first.
Laws RTA 1988 sects 2 & 3 & CUR regs 104 & 110

128. There is a danger of driver distraction being caused by in-vehicle systems such as route guidance and navigation systems, congestion warning systems, PCs, multi-media, etc. Do not operate, adjust or view any such system if it will distract your attention while you are driving; you **MUST** exercise proper control of your vehicle at all times. If necessary find a safe place to stop first.
Laws RTA 1988 sects 2 & 3 & CUR reg 104

In slow moving traffic
129. You should
- reduce the distance between you and the vehicle ahead to maintain traffic flow
- never get so close to the vehicle in front that you cannot stop safely

- leave enough space to be able to manoeuvre if the vehicle in front breaks down or an emergency vehicle needs to get past
- not change lanes to the left to overtake
- allow access into and from side roads, as blocking these will add to congestion.

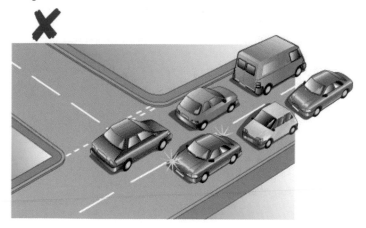

Do not block access to a side road

Driving in built-up areas

130. Narrow residential streets. You should drive slowly and carefully on streets where there are likely to be pedestrians, cyclists and parked cars. In some areas a 20 mph maximum speed limit may be in force.

Look out for
- vehicles emerging from junctions
- vehicles moving off
- car doors opening
- pedestrians
- children running out from between parked cars
- cyclists and motorcyclists.

131. Traffic calming measures. On some roads there are features such as road humps, chicanes and narrowings which are intended to slow you down. When you approach these features reduce your speed. Allow cyclists and motorcyclists room to pass through them. Maintain a reduced speed along the whole of the stretch of road within the calming measures. Give way to oncoming traffic if directed to do so by signs. You should not overtake other moving vehicles whilst in these areas.

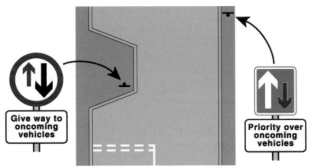

Chicanes may be used to slow traffic down

Country roads

132. Take extra care on country roads and reduce your speed at approaches to bends, which can be sharper than they appear, and at minor junctions and turnings, which may be partially hidden. Be prepared for pedestrians, horse riders and cyclists walking or riding in the road. You should also reduce your speed where country roads enter villages.

133. Single-track roads. These are only wide enough for one vehicle. They may have special passing places. If you see a vehicle coming towards you, or the driver behind wants to overtake, pull into a passing place on your left, or wait opposite a passing place on your right. Give way to vehicles coming uphill whenever you can. If necessary, reverse until you reach a passing place to let the other vehicle pass.

134. Do not park in passing places.

Using the road

General rules

135. Before moving off you should

- use all mirrors to check the road is clear
- look round to check the blind spots (the areas you are unable to see in the mirrors)
- signal if necessary before moving out
- look round for a final check.

Move off only when it is safe to do so.

Check the blind spot before moving off

136. Once moving you should

- keep to the left, unless road signs or markings indicate otherwise. The exceptions are when you want to overtake, turn right or pass parked vehicles or pedestrians in the road
- keep well to the left on right-hand bends. This will improve your view of the road and help avoid the risk of colliding with traffic approaching from the opposite direction
- keep both hands on the wheel, where possible. This will help you to remain in full control of the vehicle at all times
- be aware of other vehicles especially cycles and motorcycles. These are more difficult to see than larger vehicles and their riders are particularly vulnerable. Give them plenty of room, especially if you are driving a long vehicle or towing a trailer
- select a lower gear before you reach a long downhill slope. This will help to control your speed
- when towing, remember the extra length will affect overtaking and manoeuvring. The extra weight will also affect the braking and acceleration.

Mirrors

137. All mirrors should be used effectively throughout your journey. You should

- use your mirrors frequently so that you always know what is behind and to each side of you
- use them in good time before you signal or change direction or speed
- be aware that mirrors do not cover all areas and there will be blind spots. You will need to look round and check.

Remember: Mirrors – Signal – Manoeuvre

Overtaking

138. Before overtaking you should make sure
- the road is sufficiently clear ahead
- the vehicle behind is not beginning to overtake you
- there is a suitable gap in front of the vehicle you plan to overtake.

139. Overtake only when it is safe to do so. You should
- not get too close to the vehicle you intend to overtake
- use your mirrors, signal when it is safe to do so, take a quick sideways glance into the blind spot area and then start to move out
- not assume that you can simply follow a vehicle ahead which is overtaking; there may only be enough room for one vehicle
- move quickly past the vehicle you are overtaking, once you have started to overtake. Allow plenty of room. Move back to the left as soon as you can but do not cut in
- take extra care at night and in poor visibility when it is harder to judge speed and distance
- give way to oncoming vehicles before passing parked vehicles or other obstructions on your side of the road
- only overtake on the left if the vehicle in front is signalling to turn right, and there is room to do so
- stay in your lane if traffic is moving slowly in queues. If the queue on your right is moving more slowly than you are, you may pass on the left
- give motorcyclists, cyclists and horse riders at least as much room as you would a car when overtaking (see Rules 188, 189 and 191).

Remember: Mirrors – Signal – Manoeuvre

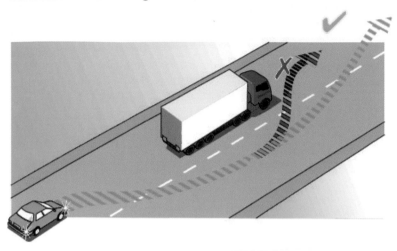

Do not cut in too quickly

140. Large vehicles. Overtaking these is more difficult.
You should
- drop back to increase your ability to see ahead. Getting too close to large vehicles will obscure your view of the road ahead and there may be another slow moving vehicle in front
- make sure that you have enough room to complete your overtaking manoeuvre before committing yourself. It takes longer to pass a large vehicle. If in doubt do not overtake
- not assume you can follow a vehicle ahead which is overtaking a long vehicle. If a problem develops, they may abort overtaking and pull back in.

141. You **MUST NOT** overtake
- if you would have to cross or straddle double white lines with a solid line nearest to you (but see Rule 108)
- if you would have to enter an area designed to divide traffic, if it is surrounded by a solid white line
- the nearest vehicle to a pedestrian crossing, especially when it has stopped to let pedestrians cross
- if you would have to enter a lane reserved for buses, trams or cycles during its hours of operation
- after a 'No Overtaking' sign and until you pass a sign cancelling the restriction.

Laws RTA 1988 sect 36, TSRGD regs 10,22,23 & 24, ZPPPCRGD reg 24

142. DO NOT overtake if there is any doubt, or where you cannot see far enough ahead to be sure it is safe. For example, when you are approaching
- a corner or bend
- a hump bridge
- the brow of a hill.

143. DO NOT overtake where you might come into conflict with other road users. For example
- approaching or at a road junction on either side of the road
- where the road narrows
- when approaching a school crossing patrol
- between the kerb and a bus or tram when it is at a stop
- where traffic is queuing at junctions or road works
- when you would force another vehicle to swerve or slow down
- at a level crossing
- when a vehicle is indicating right, even if you believe the signal should have been cancelled. Do not take a risk; wait for the signal to be cancelled.

144. Being overtaken. If a driver is trying to overtake you, maintain a steady course and speed, slowing down if necessary to let the vehicle pass. Never obstruct drivers who wish to pass. Speeding up or driving unpredictably while someone is overtaking you is dangerous. Drop back to maintain a two-second gap if someone overtakes and pulls into the gap in front of you.

145. Do not hold up a long queue of traffic, especially if you are driving a large or slow moving vehicle. Check your mirrors frequently, and if necessary, pull in where it is safe and let traffic pass.

Road junctions

146. Take extra care at junctions. You should
- watch out for cyclists, motorcyclists and pedestrians as they are not always easy to see
- watch out for pedestrians crossing a road into which you are turning. If they have started to cross they have priority, so give way
- watch out for long vehicles which may be turning at a junction ahead; they may have to use the whole width of the road to make the turn (see Rule 196)
- not assume, when waiting at a junction, that a vehicle coming from the right and signalling left will actually turn. Wait and make sure
- not cross or join a road until there is a gap large enough for you to do so safely.

147. You **MUST** stop behind the line at a junction with a 'Stop' sign and a solid white line across the road. Wait for a safe gap in the traffic before you move off.
Laws RTA 1988 sect 36 & TSRGD regs 10 & 16

148. The approach to a junction may have a 'Give Way' sign or a triangle marked on the road. You **MUST** give way to traffic on the main road when emerging from a junction with broken white lines across the road.
Laws RTA 1988 sect 36 & TSRGD regs 10(1), 16(1) & 25

149. Dual carriageways. When crossing or turning right, first assess whether the central reservation is deep enough to protect the full length of your vehicle.
*   If it is, then you should treat each half of the carriageway as a separate road. Wait in the central reservation until there is a safe gap in the traffic on the second half of the road.
*   If the central reservation is too shallow for the length of your vehicle, wait until you can cross both carriageways in one go.

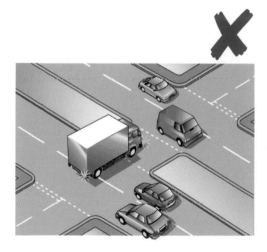

Assess your vehicle's length and do not obstruct traffic

150. Box junctions. These have criss-cross yellow lines painted on the road (see Road markings). You **MUST NOT** enter the box until your exit road or lane is clear. However, you may enter the box and wait when you want to turn right, and are only stopped from doing so by oncoming traffic, or by other vehicles waiting to turn right. At signalled roundabouts you **MUST NOT** enter the box unless you can cross over it completely without stopping.
Law TSRGD reg 10(1) & 29(2)

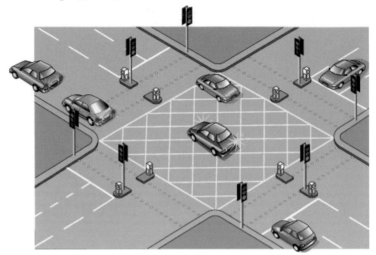

Enter a box junction only if your exit road is clear

Junctions controlled by traffic lights

151. You **MUST** stop behind the white 'Stop' line across your side of the road unless the light is green. If the amber light appears you may go on only if you have already crossed the stop line or are so close to it that to stop might cause an accident.
Laws RTA 1988 sect 36 & TSRGD regs 10 & 36

152. You **MUST NOT** move forward over the white line when the red light is showing. Only go forward when the traffic lights are green if there is room for you to clear the junction safely or you are taking up a position to turn right. If the traffic lights are not working, proceed with caution.
Laws RTA 1988 sect 36 & TSRGD regs 10 & 36

153. Green filter arrow. This indicates a filter lane only. Do not enter that lane unless you want to go in the direction of the arrow. You may proceed in the direction of the green arrow when it, or the full green light shows. Give other traffic, especially cyclists, time and room to move into the correct lane.

154. Advanced stop lines. Some junctions have advanced stop lines or bus advance areas to allow cycles and buses to be positioned ahead of other traffic. Motorists, including motorcyclists, **MUST** stop at the first white line reached, and should avoid encroaching on the marked area. If your vehicle has proceeded over the first white line at the time that the signal goes red, you **MUST** stop at the second white line, even if your vehicle is in the marked area. Allow cyclists and buses time and space to move off when the green signal shows.

Laws RTA 1988 sect 36 & TSRGD regs 10 & 43(2)

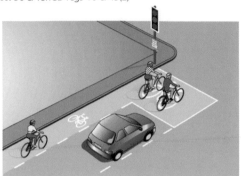

Do not encroach on the area marked for cyclists

Turning right

155. Well before you turn right you should

- use your mirrors to make sure you know the position and movement of traffic behind you
- give a right-turn signal
- take up a position just left of the middle of the road or in the space marked for traffic turning right
- leave room for other vehicles to pass on the left, if possible.

Position your vehicle correctly to avoid obstructing traffic

156. Wait until there is a safe gap between you and any oncoming vehicle. Watch out for cyclists, motorcyclists and pedestrians. Check your mirrors and blind spot again to make sure you are not being overtaken, then make the turn. Do not cut the corner. Take great care when turning into a main road; you will need to watch for traffic in both directions and wait for a safe gap.
Remember: Mirrors – Signal – Manoeuvre

157. When turning at a cross roads where an oncoming vehicle is also turning right, there is a choice of two methods
- turn right side to right side; keep the other vehicle on your right and turn behind it. This is generally the safest method as you have a clear view of any approaching traffic when completing your turn
- left side to left side, turning in front of each other. This can block your view of oncoming vehicles, so take extra care.

Road layout, markings or how the other vehicle is positioned can determine which course should be taken.

Turning right side to right side   Turning left side to left side

Turning left

158. Use your mirrors and give a left-turn signal well before you turn left. Do not overtake just before you turn left and watch out for traffic coming up on your left before you make the turn, especially if driving a large vehicle. Cyclists and motorcyclists in particular may be hidden from your view.

Do not cut in
on cyclists

159. When turning
- keep as close to the left as is safe and practical
- give way to any vehicles using a bus lane, cycle lane or tramway from either direction.

Roundabouts

160. On approaching a roundabout take notice and act on all the information available to you, including traffic signs, traffic lights and lane markings which direct you into the correct lane. You should
- use **Mirrors – Signal – Manoeuvre** at all stages
- decide as early as possible which exit you need to take
- give an appropriate signal (see Rule 162). Time your signals so as not to confuse other road users
- get into the correct lane
- adjust your speed and position to fit in with traffic conditions
- be aware of the speed and position of all the traffic around you.

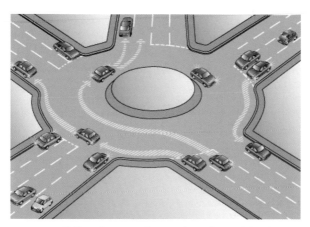

Follow the correct procedure at roundabouts

161. When reaching the roundabout you should
- give priority to traffic approaching from your right, unless directed otherwise by signs, road markings or traffic lights
- check whether road markings allow you to enter the roundabout without giving way. If so, proceed, but still look to the right before joining
- watch out for vehicles already on the roundabout; be aware they may not be signalling correctly or at all
- look forward before moving off to make sure traffic in front has moved off.

162. Signals and position, unless signs or markings indicate otherwise.

When taking the first exit
- signal left and approach in the left-hand lane
- keep to the left on the roundabout and continue signalling left to leave.

When taking any intermediate exit
- select the appropriate lane on approach to and on the roundabout, signalling where necessary
- stay in this lane until you need to alter course to exit the roundabout
- signal left after you have passed the exit before the one you want.

When taking the last exit or going full circle
- signal right and approach in the right-hand lane
- keep to the right on the roundabout until you need to change lanes to exit the roundabout
- signal left after you have passed the exit before the one you want.

When there are more than three lanes at the entrance to a roundabout, use the most appropriate lane on approach and through it.

163. In all cases watch out for and give plenty of room to
- pedestrians who may be crossing the approach and exit roads
- traffic crossing in front of you on the roundabout, especially vehicles intending to leave by the next exit
- traffic which may be straddling lanes or positioned incorrectly
- motorcyclists
- cyclists and horse riders who may stay in the left-hand lane and signal right if they intend to continue round the roundabout
- long vehicles (including those towing trailers) which might have to take a different course approaching or on the roundabout because of their length. Watch out for their signals.

164. Mini-roundabouts. Approach these in the same way as normal roundabouts. All vehicles **MUST** pass round the central markings except large vehicles which are physically incapable of doing so. Remember, there is less space to manoeuvre and less time to signal. Beware of vehicles making U-turns.

Laws RTA 1988 sect 36 & TSRGD regs 10(1) & 16(1)

165. At double mini-roundabouts treat each roundabout separately and give way to traffic from the right.

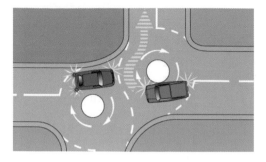

Treat each roundabout separately

166. Multiple roundabouts. At some complex junctions, there may be a series of mini-roundabouts at the intersections. Treat each mini-roundabout separately and follow the normal rules.

Pedestrian crossings

167. You **MUST NOT** park on a crossing or in the area covered by the zig-zag lines. You **MUST NOT** overtake the moving vehicle nearest the crossing or the vehicle nearest the crossing which has stopped to give way to pedestrians.

Laws ZPPPCRGD regs 18, 20 & 24, RTRA sect 25(5), TSRGD regs 10, 27 & 28

168. In queuing traffic, you should keep the crossing clear.

Keep the crossing clear

169. You should take extra care where the view of either side of the crossing is blocked by queuing traffic or incorrectly parked vehicles. Pedestrians may be crossing between stationary vehicles.

170. Allow pedestrians plenty of time to cross and do not harass them by revving your engine or edging forward.

171. Zebra crossings. As you approach a zebra crossing
- look out for people waiting to cross and be ready to slow down or stop to let them cross
- you **MUST** give way when someone has moved onto a crossing
- allow more time for stopping on wet or icy roads
- do not wave people across; this could be dangerous if another vehicle is approaching
- be aware of pedestrians approaching from the side of the crossing.

Law ZPPPCR reg 25

Signal-controlled crossings

172. Pelican crossings. These are signal-controlled crossings where flashing amber follows the red 'Stop' light. You **MUST** stop when the red light shows. When the amber light is flashing, you **MUST** give way to any pedestrians on the crossing. If the amber light is flashing and there are no pedestrians on the crossing, you may proceed with caution.

Laws ZPPPCRGD regs 23 & 26 & RTRA sect 25(5)

Allow pedestrians to cross when the amber light is flashing

173. Pelican crossings which go straight across the road are one crossing, even when there is a central island. You **MUST** wait for pedestrians who are crossing from the other side of the island.

Law ZPPPCRGD reg 26 & RTRA sect 25(5)

174. Give way to pedestrians who are still crossing after the signal for vehicles has changed to green.

175. Toucan and puffin crossings. These are similar to pelican crossings, but there is no flashing amber phase.

Reversing

176. Choose an appropriate place to manoeuvre. If you need to turn your car around, wait until you find a safe place. Try not to reverse or turn round in a busy road; find a quiet side road or drive round a block of side streets.

177. Do not reverse from a side road into a main road. When using a driveway, reverse in and drive out if you can.

178. Look carefully before you start reversing. You should
- use all your mirrors
- check the 'blind spot' behind you (the part of the road you cannot see easily in the mirrors)
- check there are no pedestrians, particularly children, cyclists, or obstructions in the road behind you
- look mainly through the rear window
- check all around just before you start to turn and be aware that the front of your vehicle will swing out as you turn
- get someone to guide you if you cannot see clearly.

Check all round when reversing

179. You **MUST NOT** reverse your vehicle further than necessary.
Law CUR reg 106

Road users requiring extra care

180. The most vulnerable road users are pedestrians, cyclists, motorcyclists and horse riders. It is particularly important to be aware of children, elderly and disabled people, and learner and inexperienced drivers and riders.

Pedestrians
181. In urban areas there is a risk of pedestrians, especially children, stepping unexpectedly into the road. You should drive with the safety of children in mind at a speed suitable for the conditions.

182. Drive carefully and slowly when
- in crowded shopping streets or residential areas
- driving past bus and tram stops; pedestrians may emerge suddenly into the road
- passing parked vehicles, especially ice cream vans; children are more interested in ice cream than traffic and may run into the road unexpectedly
- needing to cross a pavement; for example, to reach a driveway. Give way to pedestrians on the pavement
- reversing into a side road; look all around the vehicle and give way to any pedestrians who may be crossing the road
- turning at road junctions; give way to pedestrians who are already crossing the road into which you are turning
- the pavement is closed due to street repairs and pedestrians are directed to use the road.

Watch out for children in busy areas

183. Particularly vulnerable pedestrians. These include
- children and elderly pedestrians who may not be able to judge your speed and could step into the road in front of you. At 40 mph your vehicle will probably kill any pedestrians it hits. At 20 mph there is only a 1 in 20 chance of the pedestrian being killed. So kill your speed

- elderly pedestrians who may need more time to cross the road. Be patient and allow them to cross in their own time. Do not hurry them by revving your engine or edging forward
- blind and partially sighted people who may be carrying a white cane (white with a red band for deaf and blind people) or using a guide dog
- people with disabilities. Those with hearing problems may not be aware of your vehicle approaching. Those with walking difficulties require more time.

184. Near schools. Drive slowly and be particularly aware of young cyclists and pedestrians. In some places, there may be a flashing amber signal below the 'School' warning sign which tells you that there may be children crossing the road ahead. Drive very slowly until you are clear of the area.

185. Drive carefully when passing a stationary bus showing a 'School Bus' sign (see Vehicle markings) as children may be getting on or off.

186. You **MUST** stop when a school crossing patrol shows a 'Stop' for children sign (see Traffic signs).
Law RTRA sect 28

Motorcyclists and cyclists
187. It is often difficult to see motorcyclists and cyclists especially when they are coming up from behind, coming out of junctions and at roundabouts. Always look out for them when you are emerging from a junction.

Look out for motorcyclists at junctions

188. When passing motorcyclists and cyclists, give them plenty of room (see Rule 139). If they look over their shoulder whilst you are following them it could mean that they may soon attempt to turn right. Give them time and space to do so.

189. Motorcyclists and cyclists may suddenly need to avoid uneven road surfaces and obstacles such as draincovers or oily, wet or icy patches on the road. Give them plenty of room.

Other road users

190. Animals. When passing animals, drive slowly. Give them plenty of room and be ready to stop. Do not scare animals by sounding your horn or revving your engine. Look out for animals being led or ridden on the road and take extra care and keep your speed down at left-hand bends and on narrow country roads. If a road is blocked by a herd of animals, stop and switch off your engine until they have left the road. Watch out for animals on unfenced roads.

191. Horse riders. Be particularly careful of horses and riders, especially when overtaking. Always pass wide and slow. Horse riders are often children, so take extra care and remember riders may ride in double file when escorting a young or inexperienced horse rider. Look out for horse riders' signals and heed a request to slow down or stop. Treat all horses as a potential hazard and take great care.

192. Elderly drivers. Their reactions may be slower than other drivers. Make allowance for this.

193. Learners and inexperienced drivers. They may not be so skilful at reacting to events. Be particularly patient with learner drivers and young drivers. Drivers who have recently passed their test may display a 'new driver' plate or sticker.

Other vehicles

194. Emergency vehicles. You should look and listen for ambulances, fire engines, police or other emergency vehicles using flashing blue, red or green lights, headlights or sirens. When one approaches do not panic. Consider the route of the emergency vehicle and take appropriate action to let it pass. If necessary, pull to the side of the road and stop, but do not endanger other road users.

195. Powered vehicles used by disabled people. These small vehicles travel at a maximum speed of 8 mph. On a dual carriageway they **MUST** have a flashing amber light, but on other roads you may not have that advance warning.
Law RVLR reg 17(1)

196. Large vehicles. These may need extra road space to turn or to deal with a hazard that you are not able to see. If you are following a large vehicle, such as a bus or articulated lorry, be prepared to stop and wait if it needs room or time to turn.

Long vehicles need extra room

197. Large vehicles can block your view. Your ability to see and to plan ahead will be improved if you pull back to increase your separation distance.

198. Buses, coaches and trams. Give priority to these vehicles when you can do so safely, especially when they signal to pull away from stops. Look out for people getting off a bus or tram and crossing the road.

199. Electric vehicles. Be careful of electric vehicles such as milk floats and trams. Trams move quickly but silently and cannot steer to avoid you.

200. Vehicles with flashing amber lights. These warn of a slow-moving vehicle (such as a road gritter or recovery vehicle) or a vehicle which has broken down, so approach with caution.

Driving in adverse weather conditions

201. You **MUST** use headlights when visibility is seriously reduced, generally when you cannot see for more than 100 metres (328 feet). You may also use front or rear fog lights but you **MUST** switch them off when visibility improves (see Rule 211).
Law RVLR regs 25 & 27

Wet weather

202. In wet weather, stopping distances will be at least double those required for stopping on dry roads (see Rule 105 and Typical Stopping Distances diagram). This is because your tyres have less grip on the road. In wet weather

- you should keep well back from the vehicle in front. This will increase your ability to see and plan ahead
- if the steering becomes unresponsive, it probably means that water is preventing the tyres from gripping the road. Ease off the accelerator and slow down gradually
- the rain and spray from vehicles may make it difficult to see and be seen.

Icy and snowy weather

203. In winter check the local weather forecast for warnings of icy or snowy weather. **DO NOT** drive in these conditions unless your journey is essential. If it is, take great care. Carry a spade, warm clothing, a warm drink and emergency food in case your vehicle breaks down.

204. Before you set off

- you **MUST** be able to see, so clear all snow and ice from all your windows
- you **MUST** ensure that lights and number plates are clean
- make sure the mirrors are clear and the windows are de-misted thoroughly.

Laws CUR reg 30 & RVLR reg 23

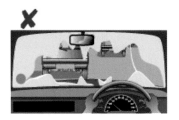 

Make sure your windscreen is completely clear

205. When driving in icy or snowy weather

- drive with care, even if the roads have been gritted
- keep well back from the vehicle in front as stopping distances can be ten times greater than on dry roads
- take care when overtaking gritting vehicles, particularly if you are riding a motorcycle
- watch out for snowploughs which may throw out snow on either side. Do not overtake them unless the lane you intend to use has been cleared
- be prepared for the road conditions changing over relatively short distances.

206. Drive extremely carefully when the roads are icy. Avoid sudden actions as these could cause a skid. You should

- drive at a slow speed in as high a gear as possible; accelerate and brake very gently
- drive particularly slowly on bends where skids are more likely. Brake progressively on the straight before you reach a bend. Having slowed down, steer smoothly round the bend, avoiding sudden actions
- check your grip on the road surface when there is snow or ice by choosing a safe place to brake gently. If the steering feels unresponsive this may indicate ice and your vehicle losing its grip on the road. When travelling on ice, tyres make virtually no noise.

Windy weather

207. High sided vehicles are most affected by windy weather, but strong gusts can also blow a car, cyclist or motorcyclist off course. This can happen at open stretches of road exposed to strong cross winds, or when passing bridges or gaps in hedges.

208. In very windy weather your vehicle may be affected by turbulence created by large vehicles. Motorcyclists are particularly affected, so keep well back from them when they are overtaking a high-sided vehicle.

Fog

209. Before entering fog check your mirrors then slow down. If the word 'Fog' is shown on a roadside signal but the road is clear, be prepared for a bank of fog or drifting patchy fog ahead. Even if it seems to be clearing, you can suddenly find yourself in thick fog.

210. When driving in fog you should

- use your lights as required in Rule 201
- keep a safe distance behind the vehicle in front. Rear lights can give a false sense of security

- be able to pull up within the distance you can see clearly.
  This is particularly important on motorways and dual carriageways,
  as vehicles are travelling faster
- use your windscreen wipers and demisters
- beware of other drivers not using headlights
- not accelerate to get away from a vehicle which is too close
  behind you
- check your mirrors before you slow down. Then use your brakes so
  that your brake lights warn drivers behind you that you are slowing
  down
- stop in the correct position at a junction with limited visibility and
  listen for traffic. When you are sure it is safe to emerge, do so
  positively and do not hesitate in a position that puts you directly in
  the path of approaching vehicles.

211. You **MUST NOT** use front or rear fog lights unless visibility is
seriously reduced (see Rule 201) as they dazzle other road users and can
obscure your brake lights. You **MUST** switch them off when visibility
improves.
Law RVLR regs 25 & 27

Hot weather
212. Keep your vehicle well ventilated to avoid drowsiness. Be aware
that the road surface may become soft or if it rains after a dry spell it
may become slippery. These conditions could affect your steering and
braking.

Waiting and parking

213. You **MUST NOT** wait or park where there are restrictions
shown by
- yellow lines along the edge of the carriageway (see Road markings)
- school entrance markings on the carriageway.
The periods when restrictions apply are shown on upright signs, usually
at intervals along the road, parallel to the kerb.
Law RTRA sects 5 & 8

Parking
214. Use off-street parking areas, or bays marked out with white lines
on the road as parking places, wherever possible. If you have to stop on
the road side

- stop as close as you can to the side
- do not stop too close to a vehicle displaying a Blue Badge, remember, they may need more room to get in or out
- you **MUST** switch off the engine, headlights and fog lights
- you **MUST** apply the handbrake before leaving the vehicle
- you **MUST** ensure you do not hit anyone when you open your door
- it is safer for your passengers (especially children) to get out of the vehicle on the side next to the kerb
- lock your vehicle.

Laws CSDPA sect 21, CUR reg 98,105 & 107, RVLR reg 27, RTA 1988 sect 42

Check before opening your door

215. You **MUST NOT** stop or park on

- the carriageway or the hard shoulder of a motorway except in an emergency (see Rule 244)
- a pedestrian crossing, including the area marked by the zig-zag lines (see Rule 167)
- a Clearway (see Traffic signs)
- a Bus Stop Clearway within its hours of operation
- taxi bays as indicated by upright signs and markings
- an Urban Clearway within its hours of operation, except to pick up or set down passengers (see Traffic signs)
- a road marked with double white lines, except to pick up or set down passengers
- a bus, tram or cycle lane during its period of operation
- a cycle track
- red lines, in the case of specially designated 'red routes', unless otherwise indicated by signs.

Laws MT(E&W)R regs 7 & 9, MT(S)R regs 6 & 8, ZPPPCRGD regs 18 & 20, RTRA sects 5 & 8, TSRGD regs 10, 26, 27 & 29(1), RTA 1988 sects 36 & 21(1)

216. You **MUST NOT** park in parking spaces reserved for specific users, such as Blue Badge holders or residents, unless entitled to do so.
Laws CSDPA sect 21 & RTRA sects 5 & 8

217. DO NOT park your vehicle or trailer on the road where it would endanger, inconvenience or obstruct pedestrians or other road users. For example, do not stop
- near a school entrance
- anywhere you would prevent access for Emergency Services
- at or near a bus stop or taxi rank
- on the approach to a level crossing
- opposite or within 10 metres (32 feet) of a junction, except in an authorised parking space
- near the brow of a hill or hump bridge
- opposite a traffic island or (if this would cause an obstruction) another parked vehicle
- where you would force other traffic to enter a tram lane
- where the kerb has been lowered to help wheelchair users
- in front of an entrance to a property
- on a bend.

218. DO NOT park partially or wholly on the pavement unless signs permit it. Parking on the pavement can obstruct and seriously inconvenience pedestrians, people in wheelchairs, the visually impaired and people with prams or pushchairs.

219. Controlled Parking Zones. The zone entry signs indicate the times when the waiting restrictions within the zone are in force. Parking may be allowed in some places at other times. Otherwise parking will be within separately signed and marked bays.

220. Goods vehicles. Vehicles with a maximum laden weight of over 7.5 tonnes (including any trailer) **MUST NOT** be parked on a verge, pavement or any land situated between carriageways, without police permission. The only exception is when parking is essential for loading and unloading, in which case the vehicle **MUST NOT** be left unattended.
Law RTA 1988 sect 19

221. Loading and unloading. Do not load or unload where there are yellow markings on the kerb and upright signs advise restrictions are in place (see Road markings). This may be permitted where parking is otherwise restricted. On red routes, specially marked and signed bays indicate where and when loading and unloading is permitted.
Law RTRA sects 5 & 8

Parking at night

222. You **MUST NOT** park on a road at night facing against the direction of the traffic flow unless in a recognised parking space.
Laws CUR reg 101 & RVLR reg 24

223. All vehicles **MUST** display parking lights when parked on a road or a lay-by on a road with a speed limit greater than 30 mph.
Law RVLR reg 24

224. Cars, goods vehicles not exceeding 1525kg unladen, invalid carriages and motorcycles may be parked without lights on a road (or lay-by) with a speed limit of 30 mph or less if they are
- at least 10 metres (32 feet) away from any junction, close to the kerb and facing in the direction of the traffic flow
- in a recognised parking place or lay-by.

Other vehicles and trailers, and all vehicles with projecting loads, **MUST NOT** be left on a road at night without lights.
Law RVLR reg 24

225. Parking in fog. It is especially dangerous to park on the road in fog. If it is unavoidable, leave your parking lights or sidelights on.

226. Parking on hills. If you park on a hill you should
- park close to the kerb and apply the handbrake firmly
- select a forward gear and turn your steering wheel away from the kerb when facing uphill
- select reverse gear and turn your steering wheel towards the kerb when facing downhill
- use 'park' if your car has an automatic gearbox.

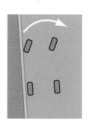

Motorways

Many other Rules apply to motorway driving, either wholly or in part: Rules 43, 67–105, 109–113, 118, 122, 126–128, 135, 137, 194, 196, 200, 201–212, 248–252, 254–264.

General

227. Prohibited vehicles. Motorways **MUST NOT** be used by pedestrians, holders of provisional car or motorcycle driving licences unless exempt, riders of motorcycles under 50cc, cyclists and horse riders. Certain slow-moving vehicles and those carrying oversized loads (except by special permission), agricultural vehicles and most invalid carriages are also prohibited.

Laws HA 1980 sects 16, 17 & sch 4, MT(E&W)R reg 4, MT(E&W)(A)R, R(S)A sects 7 ,8 & sch 3 & MT(S)R reg 10

228. Traffic on motorways usually travels faster than on other roads, so you have less time to react. It is especially important to use your mirrors earlier and look much further ahead than you would on other roads.

Motorway signals

229. Motorway signals (see Light signals controlling traffic) are used to warn you of a danger ahead. For example, there may be an accident, fog, or a spillage, which you may not immediately be able to see.

230. Signals situated on the central reservation apply to all lanes. On very busy stretches, signals may be overhead with a separate signal for each lane.

231. Amber flashing lights. These warn of a hazard ahead. The signal may show a temporary maximum speed limit, lanes that are closed or a message such as 'Fog'. Adjust your speed and look out for the danger until you pass a signal which is not flashing or one that gives the 'All clear' sign and you are sure it is safe to increase your speed.

232. Red flashing lights. If red lights on the overhead signals flash above your lane (there may also be a red 'X') you **MUST NOT** go beyond the signal in that lane. If red lights flash on a signal in the central reservation or at the side of the road, you **MUST NOT** go beyond the signal in any lane.

Laws RTA 1988 sect 36 & TSRGD regs 10 & 38

Driving on the motorway
Joining the motorway

233. When you join the motorway you will normally approach it from a road on the left (a slip road) or from an adjoining motorway. You should
- give priority to traffic already on the motorway
- check the traffic on the motorway and adjust your speed to fit safely into the traffic flow in the left-hand lane
- not cross solid white lines that separate lanes
- stay on the slip road if it continues as an extra lane on the motorway
- remain in the left-hand lane long enough to adjust to the speed of traffic before considering overtaking.

On the motorway

234. When you can see well ahead and the road conditions are good, you should
- drive at a steady cruising speed which you and your vehicle can handle safely and is within the speed limit (see Rule 103 and Speed Limits diagram)
- keep a safe distance from the vehicle in front and increase the gap on wet or icy roads, or in fog (see Rules 105 & 210).

235. You **MUST NOT** exceed 70 mph, or the maximum speed limit permitted for your vehicle (see Rule 103 and Speed Limits diagram). If a lower speed limit is in force, either permanently or temporarily, at roadworks for example, you **MUST NOT** exceed the lower limit. On some motorways, mandatory motorway signals (which display the speed within a red ring) are used to vary the maximum speed limit to improve traffic flow. You **MUST NOT** exceed this speed limit.
Law RTRA sects 17, 86, 89 & sch 6

236. The monotony of driving on a motorway can make you feel sleepy. To minimise the risk, follow the advice in Rule 80.

237. You **MUST NOT** reverse, cross the central reservation, or drive against the traffic flow. If you have missed your exit, or have taken the wrong route, carry on to the next exit.
Laws MT(E&W)R regs 6, 7 & 10 & MT(S)R regs 4, 5, 7 & 9

Lane discipline

238. You should drive in the left-hand lane if the road ahead is clear. If you are overtaking a number of slower moving vehicles it may be safer to remain in the centre or outer lanes until the manoeuvre is completed rather than continually changing lanes. Return to the left-hand lane once you have overtaken all the vehicles or if you are delaying traffic

behind you. Slow moving or speed restricted vehicles should always remain in the left-hand lane of the carriageway unless overtaking. You **MUST NOT** drive on the hard shoulder except in an emergency or if directed to do so by signs.

Laws MT(E&W)R regs 5, 9 & 16(1)(a) & MT(S)R regs 4, 8 & 14(1)(a)

239. The right-hand lane of a motorway with three or more lanes **MUST NOT** be used (except in prescribed circumstances) if you are driving

- any vehicle drawing a trailer
- a goods vehicle with a maximum laden weight over 7.5 tonnes
- a passenger vehicle with a maximum laden weight exceeding 7.5 tonnes constructed or adapted to carry more than eight seated passengers in addition to the driver.

Laws MT(E&W)R reg 12 & MT(S)R reg 11

240. Approaching a junction. Look well ahead for signals or signs. Direction signs may be placed over the road. If you need to change lanes, do so in good time. At some junctions a lane may lead directly off the motorway. Only get in that lane if you wish to go in the direction indicated on the overhead signs.

Overtaking

241. Do not overtake unless you are sure it is safe to do so. Overtake only on the right. You should

- check your mirrors
- take time to judge the speeds correctly
- make sure that the lane you will be joining is sufficiently clear ahead and behind
- take a quick sideways glance into the blind spot area to verify the position of a vehicle that may have disappeared from your view in the mirror
- remember that traffic may be coming up behind you very quickly. Check your mirrors carefully. When it is safe to do so, signal in plenty of time, then move out
- ensure you do not cut in on the vehicle you have overtaken
- be especially careful at night and in poor visibility when it is harder to judge speed and distance.

242. Do not overtake on the left or move to a lane on your left to overtake. In congested conditions, where adjacent lanes of traffic are moving at similar speeds, traffic in left-hand lanes may sometimes be moving faster than traffic to the right. In these conditions you may keep up with the traffic in your lane even if this means passing traffic in the lane to your right. Do not weave in and out of lanes to overtake.

243. You **MUST NOT** use the hard shoulder for overtaking.
Laws MT(E&W)R regs 5 & 9 & MT(S)R regs 4 & 8

Stopping

244. You **MUST NOT** stop on the carriageway, hard shoulder, slip road, central reservation or verge except in an emergency, or when told to do so by the police, an emergency sign or by flashing red light signals.
Laws MT(E&W)R regs 7(1), 9, 10 & 16 & MT(S)R regs 6(1), 8, 9 & 14

245. You **MUST NOT** pick up or set down anyone, or walk on a motorway, except in an emergency.
Laws RTRA sect 17 & MT(E&W)R reg 15

Leaving the motorway

246. Unless signs indicate that a lane leads directly off the motorway, you will normally leave the motorway by a slip road on your left. You should
- watch for the signs letting you know you are getting near your exit
- move into the left-hand lane well before reaching your exit
- signal left in good time and reduce your speed on the slip road as necessary.

247. On leaving the motorway or using a link road between motorways, your speed may be higher than you realise – 50 mph may feel like 30 mph. Check your speedometer and adjust your speed accordingly. Some slip roads and link roads have sharp bends, so you will need to slow down.

Breakdowns and accidents

Breakdowns
248. If your vehicle breaks down, think first of other road users and
- get your vehicle off the road if possible
- warn other traffic by using your hazard warning lights if your vehicle is causing an obstruction
- put a warning triangle on the road at least 45 metres (147 feet) behind your broken down vehicle on the same side of the road, or use other permitted warning devices if you have them. Always take great care when placing them, but never use them on motorways
- keep your sidelights on if it is dark or visibility is poor
- do not stand (or let anybody else stand), between your vehicle and oncoming traffic
- at night or in poor visibility do not stand where you will prevent other road users seeing your lights.

Additional rules for the motorway
249. If your vehicle develops a problem, leave the motorway at the next exit or pull into a service area. If you cannot do so, you should
- pull on to the hard shoulder and stop as far to the left as possible, with your wheels turned to the left
- try to stop near an emergency telephone (situated at approximately one mile intervals along the hard shoulder)
- leave the vehicle by the left-hand door and ensure your passengers do the same. You **MUST** leave any animals in the vehicle or, in an emergency, keep them under proper control on the verge
- do not attempt even simple repairs
- ensure that passengers keep away from the carriageway and hard shoulder, and that children are kept under control
- walk to an emergency telephone on your side of the carriageway (follow the arrows on the posts at the back of the hard shoulder)– the telephone is free of charge and connects directly to the police. Use these in preference to a mobile phone (see Rule 257)
- give full details to the police; also inform them if you are a vulnerable motorist such as a woman travelling alone
- return and wait near your vehicle (well away from the carriageway and hard shoulder)
- if you feel at risk from another person, return to your vehicle by a left-hand door and lock all doors. Leave your vehicle again as soon as you feel this danger has passed.

Laws MT(E&W)R reg 14 & MT(S)R reg 12

Keep well back from the hard shoulder

250. Before you rejoin the carriageway after a breakdown, build up speed on the hard shoulder and watch for a safe gap in the traffic. Be aware that other vehicles may be stationary on the hard shoulder.

251. If you cannot get your vehicle on to the hard shoulder
- do not attempt to place any warning device on the carriageway
- switch on your hazard warning lights
- leave your vehicle only when you can safely get clear of the carriageway.

Disabled drivers

252. If you have a disability which prevents you from following the above advice you should
- stay in your vehicle
- switch on your hazard warning lights
- display a 'Help' pennant or, if you have a car or mobile telephone, contact the emergency services and be prepared to advise them of your location.

Obstructions

253. If anything falls from your vehicle (or any other vehicle) on to the road, stop and retrieve it only if it is safe to do so.

254. Motorways. On a motorway do not try to remove the obstruction yourself. Stop at the next emergency telephone and call the police.

Accidents

255. Warning signs or flashing lights. If you see or hear emergency vehicles in the distance be aware there may be an accident ahead.

256. When passing the scene of an accident do not be distracted or slow down unnecessarily (for example if an accident is on the other side of a dual carriageway). This may cause another accident or traffic congestion, but see Rule 257.

257. If you are involved in an accident or stop to give assistance
- use your hazard warning lights to warn other traffic
- ask drivers to switch off their engines and stop smoking
- arrange for the emergency services to be called immediately with full details of the accident location and any casualties (on a motorway, use the emergency telephone which allows easy location by the emergency services. If you use a mobile phone, first make sure you have identified your location from the marker posts on the side of the hard shoulder)
- move uninjured people away from the vehicles to safety; on a motorway this should, if possible, be well away from the traffic, the hard shoulder and the central reservation
- do not move injured people from their vehicles unless they are in immediate danger from fire or explosion
- do not remove a motorcyclist's helmet unless it is essential to do so
- be prepared to give first aid as shown in Annexe 7: First aid on the road
- stay at the scene until emergency services arrive.

If you are involved in any other medical emergency on the motorway you should contact the emergency services in the same way.

Accidents involving dangerous goods

258. Vehicles carrying dangerous goods in packages will be marked with plain orange reflective plates. Road tankers and vehicles carrying tank containers of dangerous goods will have hazard warning plates (see Vehicle markings).

259. If an accident involves a vehicle containing dangerous goods, follow the advice in Rule 257 and, in particular

- switch off engines and **DO NOT SMOKE**
- keep well away from the vehicle and do not be tempted to try to rescue casualties as you yourself could become one
- call the emergency services and give as much information as possible about the labels and markings on the vehicle.
  DO NOT use a mobile phone close to a vehicle carrying flammable loads.

Documentation

260. If you are involved in an accident which causes damage or injury to any other person, vehicle, animal or property, you **MUST**

- stop
- give your own and the vehicle owner's name and address, and the registration number of the vehicle, to anyone having reasonable grounds for requiring them
- if you do not give your name and address at the time of the accident, report the accident to the police as soon as reasonably practicable, and in any case within 24 hours.

Law RTA 1988 sect 170

261. If another person is injured and you do not produce your insurance certificate at the time of the accident to a police officer or to anyone having reasonable grounds to request it, you **MUST**

- report the accident to the police as soon as possible and in any case within 24 hours
- produce your insurance certificate for the police within seven days.

Law RTA 1988 sect 170

Road works

262. When the 'Road Works Ahead' sign is displayed, you will need to be more watchful and look for additional signs providing more specific instructions.

- You **MUST NOT** exceed any temporary maximum speed limit.
- Use your mirrors and get into the correct lane for your vehicle in good time and as signs direct.
- Do not switch lanes to overtake queuing traffic.
- Do not drive through an area marked off by traffic cones.
- Watch out for traffic entering or leaving the works area, but do not be distracted by what is going on there.
- Bear in mind that the road ahead may be obstructed by the works or by slow moving or stationary traffic.

Law RTRA sect 16

Additional rules for high speed roads

263. Take special care on motorways and other high speed dual carriageways.

- One or more lanes may be closed to traffic and a lower speed limit may apply.
- Works vehicles that are slow moving or stationary with a large 'Keep Left' or 'Keep Right' sign on the back are sometimes used to close lanes for repairs.
- Check mirrors, slow down and change lanes if necessary.
- Keep a safe distance from the vehicle in front (see Rule 105).

264. Contraflow systems mean that you may be travelling in a narrower lane than normal and with no permanent barrier between you and oncoming traffic. The hard shoulder may be used for traffic, but be aware that there may be broken down vehicles ahead of you. Keep a good distance from the vehicle ahead and observe any temporary speed limits.

Railway level crossings

265. A level crossing is where a road crosses a railway line. Approach and cross it with care. Never drive on to a crossing until the road is clear on the other side and do not get too close to the car in front. Never stop or park on, or near, a crossing.

Controlled crossings

266. Most crossings have traffic light signals with a steady amber light, twin flashing red stop lights (see Light signals controlling traffic and Traffic signs) and an audible alarm for pedestrians. They may have full, half or no barriers.

- You **MUST** always obey the flashing red stop lights.
- You **MUST** stop behind the white line across the road.
- Keep going if you have already crossed the white line when the amber light comes on.
- You **MUST** wait if a train goes by and the red lights continue to flash. This means another train will be passing soon.
- Only cross when the lights go off and barriers open.
- Never zig-zag around half-barriers, they lower automatically because a train is approaching.
- At crossings where there are no barriers, a train is approaching when the lights show.

Laws RTA 1988 sect 36 & TSRGD regs 10 & 40

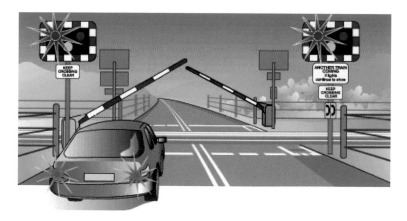

Stop when the traffic lights show

267. Railway telephones. If you are driving a large or slow-moving vehicle, or herding animals, a train could arrive before you are clear of the crossing. You **MUST** obey any sign instructing you to use the railway telephone to obtain permission to cross. You **MUST** also telephone when clear of the crossing.
Laws RTA 1988 sect 36 & TSRGD regs 10 & 16(1)

268. Crossings without traffic lights. Vehicles should stop and wait at the barrier or gate when it begins to close and not cross until the barrier or gate opens.

User-operated gates or barriers

269. Some crossings have 'Stop' signs and small red and green lights. You **MUST NOT** cross when the red light is showing, only cross if the green light is on. If crossing with a vehicle, you should

- open the gates or barriers on both sides of the crossing
- check that the green light is still on and cross quickly
- close the gates or barriers when you are clear of the crossing.

Laws RTA 1988 sect 36 & TSRGD regs 10 & 52(2)

270. If there are no lights, follow the procedure in Rule 269. Stop, look both ways and listen before you cross. If there is a railway telephone, always use it to contact the signal operator to make sure it is safe to cross. Inform the signal operator again when you are clear of the crossing.

Open crossings

271. These have no gates, barriers, attendant or traffic lights but will have a 'Give Way' sign. You should look both ways, listen and make sure there is no train coming before you cross.

Accidents and breakdowns

272. If your vehicle breaks down, or if you have an accident on a crossing you should

- get everyone out of the vehicle and clear of the crossing immediately
- use a railway telephone if available to tell the signal operator. Follow the instructions you are given
- move the vehicle clear of the crossing if there is time before a train arrives. If the alarm sounds, or the amber light comes on, leave the vehicle and get clear of the crossing immediately.

Tramways

273. You **MUST NOT** enter a road, lane or other route reserved for trams. Take extra care where trams run along the road. The width taken up by trams is often shown by tram lanes marked by white lines, yellow dots or by a different type of road surface. Diamond-shaped signs give instructions to tram drivers only.
Law RTRA sects 5 & 8

274. Take extra care where the track crosses from one side of the road to the other and where the road narrows and the tracks come close to the kerb. Tram drivers usually have their own traffic signals and may be permitted to move when you are not. Always give way to trams. Do not try to race or overtake them.

275. You **MUST NOT** park your vehicle where it would get in the way of trams or where it would force other drivers to do so.
Law RTRA sects 5 & 8

276. Tram stops. Where the tram stops at a platform, either in the middle or at the side of the road, you **MUST** follow the route shown by the road signs and markings. At stops without platforms you **MUST NOT** drive between a tram and the left-hand kerb when a tram has stopped to pick up passengers.
Law RTRA sects 5 & 8

277. Look out for pedestrians, especially children, running to catch a tram approaching a stop.

278. Cyclists and motorcyclists should take extra care when riding close to or crossing the tracks, especially if the rails are wet. It is safest to cross the tracks directly at right angles.

Light signals controlling traffic

Traffic Light Signals

RED means 'Stop'. Wait behind the stop line on the carriageway

RED AND AMBER also means 'Stop'. Do not pass through or start until GREEN shows

GREEN means you may go on if the way is clear. Take special care if you intend to turn left or right and give way to pedestrians who are crossing

AMBER means 'Stop' at the stop line. You may go on only if the AMBER appears after you have crossed the stop line or are so close to it that to pull up might cause an accident

A GREEN ARROW may be provided in addition to the full green signal if movement in a certain direction is allowed before or after the full green phase. If the way is clear you may go but only in the direction shown by the arrow. You may do this whatever other lights may be showing. White light signals may be provided for trams

Flashing red lights

Alternately flashing red lights mean YOU MUST STOP

At level crossings, lifting bridges, airfields, fire stations, etc

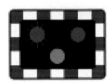

Motorway signals

Do not proceed further in this lane

Change lane

Reduced visibilty ahead

Lane ahead closed

Temporary maximum speed limit and information message

Leave motorway at next exit

Temporary maximum speed limit

End of restriction

Lane control signals

Green arrow – lane available to traffic facing the sign.
Red crosses – lane closed to traffic facing the sign.
White diagonal arrow – change lanes in direction shown.

Signals to other road users

Direction indicator signals

I intend to move out to the
right or turn right

I intend to move in to the left or
turn left or stop on the left

Brake light signals

Reversing light signals

I am applying the brakes

I intend to reverse

These signals should not be used except for the purposes described.

Arm signals

For use when direction indicator signals are not used, or when necessary to reinforce direction indicator signals and stop lights. *Also for use by pedal cyclists and those in charge of horses.*

I intend to move in to
the left or turn left

I intend to move out to
the right or turn right

I intend to slow
down or stop

Signals by authorised persons

Stop

Traffic approaching from the front

Traffic approaching from both front and behind

Traffic approaching from behind

To beckon traffic on

From the side

From the front

From behind*

Arm signals to persons controlling traffic

I want to go straight on

I want to turn left; use either hand

I want to turn right

*In Wales, bilingual signs appear on emergency services vehicles and clothing

Traffic signs

Signs giving orders

Signs with red circles are mostly prohibitive. Plates below signs qualify their message.

Entry to 20 mph zone

End of 20 mph zone

School crossing patrol

Maximum speed

National speed limit applies

Stop and give way

Give way to traffic on major road

No vehicles except bicycles being pushed

Give priority to vehicles from opposite direction

No vehicle or combination of vehicles over length shown

No vehicles over height shown

No vehicles over width shown

No goods vehicles over maximum gross weight shown (in tonnes) except for loading and unloading

No overtaking

No motor vehicles

Manually operated temporary STOP and GO signs

No buses (over 8 passenger seats)

No cycling

No towed caravans

No vehicles carrying explosives

No right turn

No left turn

No U-turns

No vehicles over maximum gross weight shown (in tonnes)

No entry for vehicular traffic

No waiting

No stopping (Clearway)

URBAN CLEARWAY
Monday to Friday

am	pm
8.00 - 9.30	4.30 - 6.30

No stopping during times shown except for as long as necessary to set down or pick up passengers

P Permit holders only

Parking restricted to permit holders

RED ROUTE
No stopping at any time except buses

No stopping during period indicated except for buses

Note: Although *The Highway Code* shows many of the signs commonly in use, a comprehensive explanation of the signing system is given in the Department's booklet *Know Your Traffic Signs*, which is on sale at booksellers. The booklet also illustrates and explains the vast majority of signs the road user is likely to encounter. The signs illustrated in *The Highway Code* are not all drawn to the same scale. In Wales, bilingual versions of some signs are used including Welsh and English versions of place names. Some older designs of signs may still be seen on the roads.

Signs with blue circles but no red border mostly give positive instruction.

One-way traffic (note: compare circular 'Ahead only' sign)

Ahead only

Turn left ahead (right if symbol reversed)

Turn left (right if symbol reversed)

Keep left (right if symbol reversed)

Route to be used by pedal cycles only

Segregated pedal cycle and pedestrian route

Minimum speed

End of minimum speed

Mini-roundabout (roundabout circulation – give way to vehicles from the immediate right)

Vehicles may pass either side to reach same destination

Buses and cycles only

Trams only

Pedestrian crossing point over tramway

With-flow bus and cycle lane

Contra-flow bus lane

With-flow pedal cycle lane

Warning signs Mostly triangular

Distance to 'STOP' line ahead

Crossroads

Junction on bend ahead

T-junction

Staggered junction

Distance to 'Give Way' line ahead

The priority through route is indicated by the broader line.

Sharp deviation of route to left (or right if chevrons reversed)

Double bend first to left (symbol may be reversed)

Bend to right (or left if symbol reversed)

Roundabout

Uneven road

Plate below some signs

Dual carriage-way ends

Road narrows on right (left if symbol reversed)

Road narrows on both sides

Two-way traffic crosses one-way road

Two-way traffic straight ahead

Traffic signals

Traffic signals not in use

Slippery road

Steep hill downwards

Steep hill upwards

Gradients may be shown as a ratio i.e. 20% = 1:5

Warning signs – continued

School crossing patrol ahead (some signs have amber lights which flash when children are crossing)

Frail (or blind or disabled if shown) pedestrians likely to cross road ahead

Pedestrians in road ahead

Pedestrian crossing

Traffic queues likely ahead

Cycle route ahead

Side winds

Hump bridge

Worded warning sign

Risk of ice

Risk of grounding

Light signals ahead at level crossing, airfield or bridge

Level crossing with barrier or gate ahead

Level crossing without barrier or gate ahead

Level crossing without barrier

Trams crossing ahead

Cattle

Wild animals

Wild horses or ponies

Accompanied horses or ponies

Quayside or river bank

Opening or swing bridge ahead

Low-flying aircraft or sudden aircraft noise

Falling or fallen rocks

Available width of headroom indicated

Overhead electric cable; plate indicates maximum height of vehicles which can pass safely

Tunnel ahead

Distance over which road humps extend

Other danger; plate indicates nature of danger

Soft verges

Direction signs Mostly rectangular

Signs on motorways – blue backgrounds

At a junction leading directly into a motorway (junction number may be shown on a black background)

On approaches to junctions (junction number on black background)

Route confirmatory sign after junction

Downward pointing arrows mean 'Get in lane'
The left-hand lane leads to a different destination from the other lanes

The panel with the inclined arrow indicates the destinations which can be reached by leaving the motorway at the next junction

Signs on primary routes – green backgrounds

On approaches to junctions

On approaches to junctions

Blue panels indicate that the motorway starts at the junction ahead.
Motorways shown in brackets can also be reached along the route indicated.
White panels indicate local or non–primary routes leading from the junction ahead.
Brown panels show the route to tourist attractions.
The name of the junction may be shown at the top of the sign.
The aircraft symbol indicates the route to an airport.
A symbol may be included to warn of a hazard or restriction along that route.

Route confirmatory sign after junction

At the junction

On approach to a junction in Wales (bilingual)

Signs on non-primary and local routes – black borders

On approaches to junctions

Green panels indicate that the primary route starts at the junction ahead. Route numbers on a blue background show the direction to a motorway. Route numbers on a green background show the direction to a primary route.

At the junction

Direction to toilets with access for the disabled

Other direction signs

Picnic site

Ancient monument in the care of English Heritage

Direction to camping and caravan site

Advisory route for lorries

Tourist attraction

Route for pedal cycles forming part of a network

Route for pedestrians

Diversion route

Recommended route for pedal cycles to place shown

Symbols showing emergency diversion route for motorway and other main road traffic

Holiday route

Direction to a car park

Information signs All rectangular

Start of motorway and point from which motorway regulations apply

Area in which cameras are used to enforce traffic regulations

Traffic has priority over oncoming vehicles

No through road for vehicles

H A & E not 24 hrs

Hospital ahead with Accident and Emergency facilities

i Tourist information

Tourist information point

End of motorway

P

Parking place for solo motorcycles

Low bridge 2 miles ahead
4.4 m 14'6"

Advance warning of restriction or prohibition ahead

'Countdown' markers at exit from motorway (each bar represents 100 yards to the exit). Green-backed markers may be used on primary routes and white-backed markers with black bars on other routes. At approaches to concealed level crossings white-backed markers with red bars may be used. Although these will be erected at equal distances the bars do not represent 100 yard intervals.

GOOD FOOD
Puddleworth ½m services
Petrol 65p

Motorway service area sign showing the operator's name

Recommended route for pedal cycles

With-flow bus lane ahead which pedal cycles and taxis may also use

Controlled ZONE
Mon - Fri
8.30 am - 6.30 pm
Saturday
8.30 am - 1.30 pm

Entrance to controlled parking zone

Zone ENDS

End of controlled parking zone

Bus lane on road at junction ahead

Appropriate traffic lanes at junction ahead

Road works signs

Road works

Loose chippings

Road works 1 mile ahead

End of road works and any temporary restrictions

Temporary hazard at road works

Temporary lane closure (the number and position of arrows and red bars may be varied according to lanes open and closed)

Lane restrictions at road works ahead

One lane crossover at contraflow road works

Signs used on the back of slow-moving or stationary vehicles warning of a lane closed ahead by a works vehicle. There are no cones on the road

Slow-moving or stationary works vehicle blocking a traffic lane. Pass in the direction shown by the arrow

Mandatory speed limit ahead

Road markings Across the carriageway

Stop line at signals or police control

Stop line at 'Stop' sign

Stop line for pedestrians at a level crossing

Give way to traffic on major road

Give way to traffic from the right at a roundabout

Give way to traffic from the right at a mini-roundabout

Along the carriageway

Edge line

Centre line
See Rule 106

Hazard warning line
See Rule 106

Double white lines
See Rules 107 and 108

Diagonal hatching
See Rule 109

Lane line
See Rule 110

Along the edge of the carriageway

Waiting restrictions

Waiting restrictions indicated by yellow lines apply to the carriageway, pavement and verge. You may stop to load or unload (unless there are also loading restrictions as described below) or while passengers board or alight. Double yellow lines mean no waiting at any time, unless there are signs that specifically indicate seasonal restrictions. The times at which the restrictions apply for other road markings are shown on nearby plates or on entry signs to controlled parking zones. If no days are shown on the signs, the restrictions are in force every day including Sundays and Bank Holidays. White bay markings and upright signs (see below) indicate where parking is allowed.

Red Route stopping controls

Red lines are used on some roads instead of yellow lines. In London the double and single red lines used on Red Routes indicate that stopping to park, load/unload or to board and alight from a vehicle (except for a licensed taxi or if you hold a Blue Badge) is prohibited. The red lines apply to the carriageway, pavement and verge. The times that the red line prohibitions apply are shown on nearby signs, but the double red line ALWAYS means no stopping at any time. On Red Routes you may stop to park, load/unload in specially marked boxes and adjacent signs specify the times and purposes and duration allowed. A box MARKED IN RED indicates that it may only be available for the purpose specified for part of the day (eg between busy peak periods). A box MARKED IN WHITE means that it is available throughout the day.

RED AND SINGLE YELLOW LINES CAN ONLY GIVE A GUIDE TO THE RESTRICTIONS AND CONTROLS IN FORCE AND SIGNS, NEARBY OR AT A ZONE ENTRY, MUST BE CONSULTED.

No waiting at any time

No waiting during times shown on sign

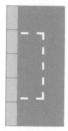

Waiting is limited to the times and duration shown

No stopping at any time

No stopping during times shown on sign

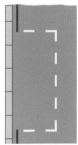

Parking is limited at the times for duration shown

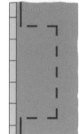

Only loading may take place at the times shown for up to a maximum duration of 20 minutes

On the kerb or at the edge of the carriageway

Loading restrictions on roads other than Red Routes

Yellow marks on the kerb or at the edge of the carriageway indicate that loading or unloading is prohibited at the times shown on the nearby black and white plates. You may stop while passengers board or alight. If no days are indicated on the signs the restrictions are in force every day including Sundays and Bank Holidays. ALWAYS CHECK THE TIMES SHOWN ON THE PLATES.

Lengths of road reserved for vehicles loading and unloading are indicated by a white 'bay' marking with the words 'Loading Only' and a sign with the white on blue 'trolley' symbol. This sign also shows whether loading and unloading is restricted to goods vehicles and the times at which the bay can be used. If no times or days are shown it may be used at any time. Vehicles may not park here if they are not loading or unloading.

No loading or unloading at any time

No loading or unloading at the times shown

Loading bay

Other road markings

Keep entrance clear of stationary vehicles, even if picking up or setting down children

Warning of 'Give Way' just ahead

Parking space reserved for vehicles named

See Rule 215

See rule 120

Box junction See Rule 150

Do not block that part of the carriageway indicated

Indication of traffic lanes

Vehicle markings

Large goods vehicle rear markings

Motor vehicles over 7500 kilograms maximum gross weight and trailers over 3500 kilograms maximum gross weight

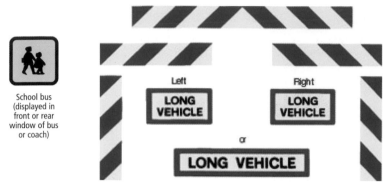

School bus (displayed in front or rear window of bus or coach)

Left — **LONG VEHICLE**

Right — **LONG VEHICLE**

or

LONG VEHICLE

The vertical markings are also required to be fitted to builders' skips placed in the road, commercial vehicles or combinations longer than 13 metres (optional on combinations between 11 and 13 metres)

Hazard warning plates

Certain tank vehicles carrying dangerous goods must display hazard information panels

2YE
1089
Newtown-on-Moors
(0123) 45678

The above panel will be displayed by vehicles carrying certain dangerous goods in packages

The panel illustrated is for flammable liquid. Diamond symbols indicating other risks include:

Toxic substance

Oxidizing substance

Non-flammable compressed gas

Radioactive substance

Spontaneously combustible substance

Corrosive substance

Projection markers

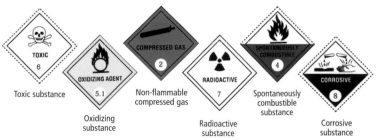

Side marker

End marker

Both required when load or equipment (eg crane jib) overhangs front or rear by more than two metres

Annexes

1. Choosing and maintaining your bicycle

Make sure that

- you choose the right size of cycle for comfort and safety
- lights and reflectors are kept clean and in good working order
- tyres are in good condition and inflated to the pressure shown on the tyre
- gears are working correctly
- the chain is properly adjusted and oiled
- the saddle and handlebars are adjusted to the correct height.

You **MUST**

- ensure your brakes are efficient
- at night, use lit front and rear lights and have an efficient red rear reflector.

PCUR regs 6 & 10 RVLR no 18

2. Motorcycle licence requirements

If you have a provisional motorcycle licence, you **MUST** satisfactorily complete a Compulsory Basic Training (CBT) course. You can then ride on the public road, with L plates (in Wales either D plates, L plates or both can be used), for up to two years. To obtain your full motorcycle licence you **MUST** pass a motorcycle theory test and then a practical test.

Law RTA 1988 sect 97

If you have a full car licence you may ride motorcycles up to 125cc and 11kW power output, with L plates (and/or D plates in Wales), on public roads, but you **MUST** first satisfactorily complete a CBT course if you have not already done so.

If you have a full moped licence and wish to obtain full motorcycle entitlement you will be required to take a motorcycle theory test if you did not take a separate theory test when you obtained your moped licence. You **MUST** then pass a practical motorcycle test.

Note that if CBT was completed for the full moped licence there is no need to repeat it, but if the moped test was taken before

1/12/90 CBT will need to be completed before riding a motorcycle as a learner.

Law MV(DL)R reg 42(1) & 69(1)

Light motorcycle licence (A1): you take a test on a motorcycle of between 75 and 125cc. If you pass you may ride a motorcycle up to 125cc with power output up to 11kW.

Standard motorcycle licence (A): if your test vehicle is between 120 and 125cc and capable of more than 100 km/h you will be given a standard (A) licence. You will then be restricted to motorcycles of up to 25 kW for two years. After two years you may ride any size machine.

Direct or Accelerated Access enables riders over the age of 21, or those who reach 21 before their two-year restriction ends, to ride larger motorcycles sooner. To obtain a licence to do so they are required to

- have successfully completed a CBT course
- pass a theory test, if they are required to do so
- pass a practical test on a machine with power output of at least 35kW.

To practise, they can ride larger motorcycles, with L plates (and/or D plates in Wales), on public roads, but only when accompanied by an approved instructor on another motorcycle in radio contact.

You **MUST NOT** carry a pillion passenger or pull a trailer until you have passed your test.

Law MV(DL)R reg 16

Moped Licence Requirements

Mopeds are up to 50cc with a maximum speed of 50 km/h.

To ride a moped, learners **MUST**
- be 16 or over
- have a provisional moped licence
- complete CBT training.

You **MUST** first pass the theory test for motorcycles and then the moped practical test to obtain your full moped licence.

If you passed your driving test before 1 February 2001 you are qualified to ride a moped without L plates (and/or D plates in Wales), although it is recommended that you complete CBT before riding on the road. If you passed your driving test after this date you **MUST** complete CBT before riding a moped on the road.

Laws MV(DL)R reg 43

Note. For motorcycle and moped riders wishing to upgrade, the following give exemption from taking the motorcycle theory test
* full A1 motorcycle licence
* full moped licence, if gained after 1/7/96.

Laws MV(DL)R reg 42

3. Motor vehicle documentation and learner driver requirements

Documents

Driving Licence. You **MUST** have a valid signed driving licence for the category of vehicle you are driving. You **MUST** inform the Driver and Vehicle Licensing Agency (DVLA) if you change your name and address.

Law RTA 1988 sect 87

Insurance. You **MUST** have a valid insurance certificate covering you for third party liability. Before driving any vehicle, make sure that it has this cover for your use or that your own insurance gives you adequate cover. You **MUST NOT** drive a vehicle without insurance.

Law RTA 1988 sect 143

MOT. Cars and motorcycles **MUST** normally pass an MOT test three years from the date of the first registration and every year after that. You **MUST NOT** drive a vehicle without an MOT certificate, when it should have one. Driving an unroadworthy vehicle may invalidate your insurance. Exceptionally, you may drive to a pre-arranged test appointment or to a garage for repairs required for the test.

Law RTA 1988 sects 45, 47, 49 & 53

Vehicle Registration Document. Registration documents are issued for all motor vehicles used on the road, describing them (make, model, etc.) and giving details of the registered keeper.

You **MUST** notify the Driver and Vehicle Licensing Agency in Swansea as soon as possible when you buy or sell a vehicle, or if you change your name or address. For registration documents issued after 27 March 1997 the buyer and seller are responsible for completing the registration documents. The seller is responsible for forwarding them to DVLA. The procedures are explained on the back of the registration documents.
Law RV(R&L)R regs 10, 12 & 13

Vehicle Excise Duty. All vehicles used or kept on the roads **MUST** have a valid Vehicle Excise Duty disc (tax disc) displayed at all times. Any vehicle exempt from duty **MUST** display a nil licence.
Law VERA sect 29

Production of documents. You **MUST** be able to produce your driving licence and counterpart, a valid insurance certificate and (if appropriate) a valid MOT certificate, when requested by a police officer. If you cannot do this you may be asked to take them to a police station within seven days.
Law RTA 1988 sects 164 & 165

Learner drivers

Learners driving a car **MUST** hold a valid provisional licence. They **MUST** be supervised by someone at least 21 years old who holds a full EC/EEA licence for that type of car (automatic or manual) and has held one for at least three years.
MV(DL)R reg 16

Vehicles. Any vehicle driven by a learner **MUST** display red L plates. In Wales, either red D plates, red L plates, or both, can be used. Plates **MUST** conform to legal specifications and **MUST** be clearly visible to others from in front of the vehicle and from behind. Plates should be removed or covered when not being driven by a learner (except on driving school vehicles).
Law MV(DL)R reg 16 & sched 4

You **MUST** pass the theory test (if one is required) and then a practical driving test for the category of vehicle you wish to drive before driving unaccompanied.
Law MV(DL)R reg 40

4. The road user and the law

Road traffic law

The following list can be found abbreviated throughout the Code. It is not intended to be a comprehensive guide, but a guide to some of the important points of law. For the precise wording of the law, please refer to the various Acts and Regulations (as amended) indicated in the Code. Abbreviations are listed below.

Most of the provisions apply on all roads throughout Great Britain, although there are some exceptions. The definition of a road in England and Wales is 'any highway and any other road to which the public has access and includes bridges over which a road passes'. In Scotland, there is a similar definition which is extended to include any way over which the public have a right of passage. It is important to note that references to 'road' therefore generally include footpaths, bridle-ways and cycle tracks and many roadways and driveways on private land (including many car parks). In most cases, the law will apply to them and there may be additional rules for particular paths or ways. Some serious driving offences, including drink-driving offences, also apply to all public places, for example public car parks.

Chronically Sick & Disabled Persons Act 1970	CSDPA
Functions of Traffic Wardens Order 1970	FTWO
Highway Act 1835 or 1980 (as indicated)	HA
Horses (Protective Headgear for Young Riders) Regulations 1992	H(PHYR)R
Motor Cycles (Protective Helmets) Regulations 1980	MC(PH)R
Motorways Traffic (England & Wales) Regulations 1982	MT(E&W)R
Motorways Traffic (Scotland) Regulations 1995	MT(S)R
Motor Vehicles (Driving Licences) Regulations 1999	MV(DL)R
Motor Vehicles (Wearing of Seat Belts) Regulations 1993	MV(WSB)R
Motor Vehicles (Wearing of Seat Belts by Children in Front Seats) Regulations 1993	MV(WSBCFS)R
Pedal Cycles (Construction & Use) Regulations 1983	PCUR
Public Passenger Vehicles Act 1981	PPVA
Road Traffic Act 1988 or 1991 (as indicated)	RTA
Road Traffic (New Drivers) Act 1995	RT(ND)A
Road Traffic Regulation Act 1984	RTRA
Road Vehicles (Construction & Use) Regulations 1986	CUR
Road Vehicles Lighting Regulations 1989	RVLR
Road Vehicles (Registration & Licensing) Regulations 1971	RV(R&L)R
Roads (Scotland) Act 1984	R(S)A
Traffic Signs Regulations & General Directions 2002	TSRGD
Vehicle Excise and Registration Act 1994	VERA
Zebra, Pelican and Puffin Pedestrian Crossings Regulations and General Directions 1997	ZPPPCRGD

5. Penalties

Parliament has set the maximum penalties for road traffic offences. The seriousness of the offence is reflected in the maximum penalty. It is for the courts to decide what sentence to impose according to circumstances.

The penalty table, see over, indicates some of the main offences, and the associated penalties. There is a wide range of other more specific offences which, for the sake of simplicity, are not shown here.

The penalty points and disqualification system is described below.

Penalty points and disqualification

The penalty point system is intended to deter drivers from following unsafe driving practices. The court **MUST** order points to be endorsed on the licence according to the fixed number or the range set by Parliament. The accumulation of penalty points acts as a warning to drivers that they risk disqualification if further offences are committed.

A driver who accumulates 12 or more penalty points within a three year period must be disqualified. This will be for a minimum period of six months, or longer if the driver has previously been disqualified.

For every offence which carries penalty points the court has a discretionary power to order the licence holder to be disqualified. This may be for any period the court thinks fit, but will usually be between a week and a few months.

In the case of serious offences, such as dangerous driving and drink-driving, the court **MUST** order disqualification. The minimum period is 12 months, but for repeat offenders or where the alcohol level is high, it may be longer. For example, a second drink-drive offence in the space of 10 years will result in a minimum of three years' disqualification.

Furthermore, in some serious cases, the court **MUST** (in addition to imposing a fixed period of disqualification) order the offender to be disqualified until they pass a driving test. In other cases the court has a discretionary power to order such disqualification. The test may be an ordinary length test or an extended test according to the nature of the offence.

Laws RTRA sects.28,29,34,35 and 36

Penalty table

Offence	Maximum penalties			
	IMPRISONMENT	FINE	DISQUALIFICATION	PENALTY POINTS
*Causing death by dangerous driving	10 years	Unlimited	Obligatory– 2 years minimum	3–11 (if exceptionally not disqualified)
*Dangerous driving	2 years	Unlimited	Obligatory	3–11 (if exceptionally not disqualified)
Causing death by careless driving under the influence of drink or drugs	10 years	Unlimited	Obligatory– 2 years minimum	3–11 (if exceptionally not disqualified)
Careless or inconsiderate driving	-	£2,500	Discretionary	3–9
Driving while unfit through drink or drugs or with excess alcohol; or failing to provide a specimen for analysis	6 months	£5,000	Obligatory	3–11 (if exceptionally not disqualified)
Failing to stop after an accident or failing to report an accident	6 months	£5,000	Discretionary	5–10
Driving when disqualified	6 months (12 months in Scotland)	£5,000	Discretionary	6
Driving after refusal or revocation of licence on medical grounds	6 months	£5,000	Discretionary	3–6
Driving without insurance	-	£5,000	Discretionary	6–8
Driving otherwise than in accordance with a licence	-	£1,000	Discretionary	3–6
Speeding	-	£1,000 (£2,500 for motorway offences)	Discretionary	3–6 or 3 (fixed penalty)
Traffic light offences	-	£1,000	Discretionary	3
No MOT certificate	-	£1,000	-	-
Seat belt offences	-	£500	-	-
Dangerous cycling	-	£2,500	-	-
Careless cycling	-	£1,000	-	-
Cycling on pavement	-	£500	-	-
Failing to identify driver of a vehicle	-	£1,000	Discretionary	3

* Where a court disqualifies a person on conviction for one of these offences, it must order an extended retest. The courts also have discretion to order a retest for any other offence which carries penalty points: an extended retest where disqualification is obligatory, and an ordinary test where disqualification is not obligatory.

New drivers. Special rules apply to drivers within two years of the date of passing their driving test if they passed the test after 1 June 1997 and held nothing but a provisional (learner) licence before passing the test. If the number of penalty points on their licence reaches six or more as a result of offences they commit before the two years are over (including any they committed before they passed the test), their licence will be revoked. They must then reapply for a provisional licence and may drive only as learners until they pass a theory and practical driving test.
Law RT(ND)A

Note. This applies even if they pay by fixed penalty. Drivers who already have a full licence for one type of vehicle are not affected by this when they pass a test to drive another type.

Other consequences of offending

Where an offence is punishable by imprisonment then the vehicle used to commit the offence may be confiscated.

In addition to the penalties a court may decide to impose, the cost of insurance is likely to rise considerably following conviction for a serious driving offence. This is because insurance companies consider such drivers are more likely to have an accident.

Drivers disqualified for drinking and driving twice within 10 years, or once if they are over two and a half times the legal limit, or those who refused to give a specimen, also have to satisfy the Driver and Vehicle Licensing Agency's Medical Branch that they do not have an alcohol problem and are otherwise fit to drive before their licence is returned at the end of their period of disqualification. Persistent misuse of drugs or alcohol may lead to the withdrawal of a driving licence.

6. Vehicle maintenance, safety and security

Vehicle maintenance

Take special care that lights, brakes, steering, exhaust system, seat belts, demisters, wipers and washers are all working. Also
- lights, indicators, reflectors, and number plates **MUST** be kept clean and clear
- windscreens and windows **MUST** be kept clean and free from obstructions to vision

- lights **MUST** be properly adjusted to prevent dazzling other road users. Extra attention needs to be paid to this if the vehicle is heavily loaded
- exhaust emissions **MUST NOT** exceed prescribed levels
- ensure your seat, seat belt, head restraint and mirrors are adjusted correctly before you drive
- items of luggage are securely stowed.

Law: many regulations within CUR cover the above equipment and RVLR regs 23 & 27

Warning displays

Make sure that you understand the meaning of all warning displays on the vehicle instrument panel. Do not ignore warning signs, they could indicate a dangerous fault developing.

- When you turn the ignition key, warning lights will be illuminated but will go out when the engine starts (except the handbrake warning light). If they do not, or if they come on whilst you are driving, stop and investigate the problem, as you could have a serious fault.
- If the charge warning light comes on while you are driving, it may mean that the battery isn't charging. This must also be checked as soon as possible to avoid loss of power to lights and other electrical systems.

Tyres

Tyres **MUST** be correctly inflated and be free from certain cuts and other defects.

Cars, light vans and light trailers MUST have a tread depth of at least 1.6mm across the central three-quarters of the breadth of the tread and around the entire circumference.

Motorcycles, large vehicles and passenger carrying vehicles MUST have a tread depth of at least 1mm across three-quarters of the breadth of the tread and in a continuous band around the entire circumference.

Mopeds should have visible tread.

Laws CUR reg 27

If a tyre bursts while you are driving, try to keep control of your vehicle. Grip the steering wheel firmly and allow the vehicle to roll to a stop at the side of the road.

If you have a flat tyre, stop as soon as it is safe to do so. Only change the tyre if you can do so without putting yourself or others at risk – otherwise call a breakdown service.

Tyre pressures. Check weekly. Do this before your journey, when tyres are cold. Warm or hot tyres may give a misleading reading.

Your brakes and steering will be adversely affected by under-inflated or over-inflated tyres. Excessive or uneven tyre wear may be caused by faults in the braking or suspension systems, or wheels which are out of alignment. Have these faults corrected as soon as possible.

Fluid levels

Check the fluid levels in your vehicle at least weekly. Low brake fluid may result in brake failure and an accident. Make sure you recognise the low fluid warning lights if your vehicle has them fitted.

Before winter

Ensure that the battery is well maintained and that there are appropriate anti-freeze agents in your radiator and windscreen bottle.

Other problems

If your vehicle

- pulls to one side when braking, it is most likely to be a brake fault or incorrectly inflated tyres. Consult a garage or mechanic immediately
- continues to bounce after pushing down on the front or rear, its shock absorbers are worn. Worn shock absorbers can seriously affect the operation of a vehicle and should be replaced
- smells of anything unusual such as burning rubber, petrol or electrical; investigate immediately. Do not risk a fire.

Overheated engines or fire

Most engines are water cooled. If your engine overheats you should wait until it has cooled naturally. Only then remove the coolant filler cap and add water or other coolant.

If your vehicle catches fire, get the occupants out of the vehicle quickly and to a safe place. Do not attempt to extinguish a fire in the engine compartment, as opening the bonnet will make the fire flare. Call the fire brigade.

Petrol stations

Never smoke or use a mobile phone on the forecourt of petrol stations as these are major fire risks and could cause an explosion.

Vehicle security

When you leave your vehicle you should
- remove the ignition key and engage the steering lock
- lock the car, even if you only leave it for a few minutes
- close the windows completely
- never leave children or pets in an unventilated car
- take all contents with you, or lock them in the boot. Remember, for all a thief knows a carrier bag may contain valuables. Never leave vehicle documents in the car.

For extra security fit an anti-theft device such as an alarm or immobiliser. If you are buying a new car it is a good idea to check the level of built-in security features. Consider having your registration number etched on all your car windows. This is a cheap and effective deterrent to professional thieves.

7. First aid on the road

In the event of an accident, you can do a number of things to help, even if you have had no training

1. Deal with danger

Further collisions and fire are the main dangers following an accident. Approach any vehicle involved with care. Switch off all engines and, if possible, warn other traffic. Stop anyone from smoking.

2. Get help

Try to get the assistance of bystanders. Get someone to call the appropriate emergency services as soon as possible. They will need to know the exact location of the accident and the number of vehicles involved.

3. Help those involved

DO NOT move casualties still in vehicles unless further danger is threatened. **DO NOT** remove a motorcyclist's helmet unless it is essential. **DO NOT** give the casualty anything to eat or drink.

DO try to make them comfortable and prevent them from getting cold, but avoid unnecessary movement. **DO** give reassurance confidently to the casualty. They may be shocked but prompt treatment will minimise this.

4. Provide emergency care
Follow the **ABC of First aid**

A is for **Airway** – check for and relieve any obstruction to breathing. Remove any obvious obstruction in the mouth. Breathing may begin and colour improve.

B is for **Breathing** – if breathing does not begin when the airway has been cleared, lift the chin and tilt the head very gently backwards. Pinch the casualty's nostrils and blow into the mouth until the chest rises; withdraw, then repeat regularly once every four seconds until the casualty can breathe unaided.

C is for **Circulation** – prevent blood loss to maintain circulation. If bleeding is present apply firm hand pressure over the wound, preferably using some clean material, without pressing on any foreign body in the wound. Secure a pad with a bandage or length of cloth. Raise the limb to lessen the bleeding, provided it is not broken.

5. Be prepared
Always carry a first aid kit. You could save a life by learning emergency aid and first aid from a qualified organisation, such as the local ambulance services, the St John Ambulance Association and Brigade, St Andrew's Ambulance Association, the British Red Cross or any suitable qualified body.

This Code, between rules 1 and 278, is issued with the Authority of Parliament (laid before both Houses of Parliament June 1998) and appears in the law described as follows:

A failure on the part of a person to observe any provision of **The Highway Code** shall not of itself render that person liable to criminal proceedings of any kind, but any such failure may in any proceedings (whether civil or criminal and including proceedings for an offence under the Traffic Acts, the Public Passenger Vehicles Act 1981 or sections 18 to 23 of the Transport Act 1985) be relied upon by any party to the proceedings as tending to establish or negative any liability which is in question in those proceedings.

Road Traffic Act 1988

Index

References are to rule numbers, except those numbers given in *bold italic*, which refer to the annexes